THE MIRACLE OF FATIMA MANSIONS

AN ESCAPE FROM DRUG ADDICTION

by Shay Byrne

maverick
house

Published by Maverick House, Main Street, Dunshaughlin, Co. Meath, Ireland.
Maverick House Asia, Level 41, 323 United Centre Building, Silom Road, Bangrak, Bangkok 10500, Thailand.

www.maverickhouse.com
email: info@maverickhouse.com

ISBN: 978-1-905379-40-8

Printed and bound by ColourBooks Ltd.

5 4 3 2 1

The paper used in this book comes from wood pulp of managed forests. For every tree felled at least one tree is planted, thereby renewing natural resources.

A CIP catalogue record for this book is available from the British Library.

DEDICATION

Dedicated to my father James (Jim) Byrne, the busiest guardian angel in Heaven.

Acknowledgements

I would like to thank the following people, without whom this book would not have been written.

Jodie, I hope you made it.

My wife Ute, thank you for gifting me two beautiful boys, and for sticking by me through some very difficult times.

Thanks also to my parents-in-law, Otto and Erika Liebisch. To my brothers and sisters; Peter, Liz, Christine, Joe, Anne and Johnny. Special thanks to Joe for allowing me to use one of his poems in the book. A debt of gratitude is owed to my loving mother, Mary Byrne, for being there for me through good times and bad.

Thanks to Michi Ploog and his ex-wife Petra, who encouraged me greatly, and to Colette O' Rourke for her support and encouragement. Thanks also to my ex-colleague Sheila Knowles for help with the initial editing, to Johnny (Chock) O' Brien of Finnegan's in Nüremberg, for being there when I needed him, and to Dietmar Dworazik and his wife Claudia for a spontaneous act of kindness.

Thank you, my sister-in-law Elke Berger, my cousin Tom Sweeney, and my nephew Simon Foley.

Thanks to the staff and residents at Coolmine Lodge, and to Ciaran Kelly, RIP, who saw out his life as a counsellor helping others to help themselves.

I'm sure there are many more, but to anyone I've forgotten, sorry, and thanks for the support, help and encouragement.

PREFACE

In early January 2007, Joe Duffy presented a programme on *RTE* television; *2006—How Was it For You?* In an item on drugs and crime, Senator David Norris had this to say: 'Well, the record drugs seizures (in Ireland in 2006) are a record waste of time. The War on Drugs is about as useful as the War on Terror. We've had seizures of cannabis and heroin, but it hasn't stopped anything. It has proliferated, it has grown out of all proportion because of the enormous profits to be made and it has introduced—The Gun! Looking at the possibility of legalising and controlling drugs; that is the only way forward. The drug seizures are a headline, they make people feel positive, but quite honestly, it is a complete and utter waste of time. It is a red herring.'

Later, Gay Byrne became embroiled in controversy when he too suggested that consideration should be given to legalising drugs.

Whether this could be a viable option or not, it does seem that conventional strategies have failed. In the early days of my descent into a life of drug dependency, I and my peers were eager and enthusiastic participants in what could be described as a cottage industry, compared to the billion-plus euro business of today. The business is now ruthlessly controlled by vicious gangs who will stop at nothing to maintain control over their domains.

For example, two of these gangs in the Drimnagh and Crumlin area where I grew up are engaged in a feud that has so far claimed nine lives. In 2006 there were 24 gun homicides in the 26 counties, most of which occurred in Dublin. The capital's murder rate is soaring due to an upsurge in gangland violence according to 'The Best of Times?'—a study by the Economic and Social Research Institute (ESRI). It revealed that Dublin's homicide rate is increasing faster than that any other European capital city. What is even more frightening is that a staggering 85% of gun murders in Ireland do not result in a conviction.

A number of these murders have been ordered and directed from prisons. A recent search of Portlaoise Prison, Ireland's maximum security jail, recovered 17 mobiles, 5 SIM cards, drugs, syringes, bootleg alcohol, and two budgies. Can anybody be in doubt that the situation is out of control?

Surely there is nothing to lose in trying an alternative to the present strategy which seems to confer even more wealth, power and influence on criminal gangs. Michael McDowell, the former Minister for Justice, is on record as stating that the drugs gangs pose as significant a threat to the State as paramilitarism did during the troubles in the North. Why not take control of the supply of drugs away from them?

Far greater resources need to be diverted into efforts aimed at rehabilitating addicts. Can any strategy which provides for 24 detox beds in a city with an estimated 13,000 heroin addicts be considered meaningful? Meanwhile, Coolmine and other rehabilitation projects constantly struggle for funding.

When I told my uncle Christy the title for my book, he replied, 'I hate Fatima Mansions!' My father's family came from a community close to Fatima Mansions, and Christy associates it with the destruction of his 'lovely Rialto'. I was not from Fatima Mansions, but events there made me realise how far I had descended into the abyss and how terrible the consequences were. I survived. Not so lucky was a friend of mine from Drimnagh, who was stabbed there. His name was Joey Sutcliffe.

In summing up the sentencing of his killer, Justice Paul Carney said that many of those present on the night he met his death 'had subsequently died of drug-related conditions in the time it took the case to come to trial.'

He spoke of the young women who 'ply their trade' on Baggot Street and Benburb Street, 'until they get enough money to buy drugs at Fatima Mansions.'

On the conclusion of the case, Judge Carney said he was 'haunted by the conditions of the cruelly named Fatima Mansions.'

My story is not a social commentary, but rather a personal struggle. As I write, however, I am aware that a major urban regeneration project is underway at the Mansions. There is a similar, larger project underway in Ballymun, another area synonymous with drugs, crime, neglect and a lack of opportunity.

Will their problems be solved by building new housing? While the construction of Ballymun and Fatima in the 1950s and 1960s must have signalled the dawn of a new era for the residents, their early promise went unfulfilled. I fear that in failing to tackle the inequality inherent in our society we are doomed to repeat the mistakes of the past, but at a new address.

– Shay Byrne, 2007

Chapter 1

It was hours since my last hit, and I was on edge, to say the least. The heroin buzz was fading, leaving behind an empty longing for more, drowning out my own body's cries for help, to stop this madness, stop polluting myself with that poison.

I didn't know what to expect in a drug treatment facility, and in particular this place, Coolmine Therapeutic Community, except what I had heard on the streets; but anything would be better than what I'd been experiencing in the 12 months leading to this day.

As I sat on the bench facing the wall, listening to the buzz of work and shouted commands, I didn't feel too bad physically, just yet; not surprising really, as I was still a little bit stoned. But I could feel it drain away bit by bit, and I knew that was all there was going to be; there would be no more.

The rule was that everyone had to be detoxed before going in, and when I had presented myself at the clinic that morning, for my initial interview, I was sure that the end result would be a two-week stay in Jervis Street Hospital for a detox, followed by a trip out to Coolmine to be 'cured'.

I had gone to the interview with *Jodie*, my girlfriend, and a couple of other junkies, *Mark* and *Bob*, having spent the whole night trying to score. We had finally scored early in the morning and I was ready for anything when I got there, cocooned as I was from the harsh realities of the real world. I was in 'Noddyland' when I first arrived. So to speak.

I was playing out the little charade, dying for the interview to be over so I could get out of there and have another turn-on, when the two guys conducting the interview asked me if I was prepared to enter therapy immediately. I told them that I was, convinced that I would first have to do a detox, which would give me time to adjust and maybe even time enough to get stoned a couple more times.

Those couple of weeks would also give me time to say goodbye to *Jodie*, who had been financing my habit by selling herself in Fitzwilliam Square, the red light district of Dublin. She was a hooker when I met her, an orphan girl from Derry. Then she'd had the misfortune to meet me, and since that fateful day she'd spent every penny she made on me.

But it was not to be; there was no two week waiting period for me, no chance to score again 'for old time's sake', and no chance of going through a more comfortable detox. My two interviewers told me I had five minutes and they would be out to collect me.

Jodie was stunned when I told her. She asked when she could visit and what I would do for clothes. It wasn't going to be like when I was in The Joy—Mountjoy Prison in Dublin—a few months earlier and she had delivered gear to me every day while I was on remand. They were the best wares, or kisses, I ever had: a condom full of gear being passed from her mouth to mine under the pretence of romance. I knew there was no way I was going to go through cold turkey in there.

She started to cry hysterically, telling me how she'd miss me and asking how she'd get by without me, and she was still in a heap, being comforted by *Mark* and *Bob*, as I was driven off in the van with the two guys from the therapy centre. She'd be fine without me; probably even better off than with me, until she found some other junkie to help bleed her dry. I knew I'd miss her, but I wasn't sure if it was because she was my girlfriend or because she was a good source of money.

Little did I know I'd never see her again. I heard later that she too had been seduced by heroin, and had become a junkie. After a while, I guess it was all she knew, and finally gave in to the inevitable.

There was a kind of love between us, as much as is possible between a hooker and a junkie, and I hope that she made it to some kind of treatment before succumbing to one of the plagues associated with being a heroin addict— AIDS, hepatitis, Septicaemia, abscesses, overdose—a whole myriad of things to be cured before beginning the cure.

My two interviewers had been friendly and chatty on the way out in the bus but as soon as we got inside the door, they became very assertive and told me to sit on a bench facing the wall.

So there I sat, on the bench facing the wall like a little kid at school. All that was missing was the dunce's cap. I started to read the rules:

1. There will be no violence or threats of violence.

2. There will be no use of drugs, chemicals, or alcohol. Anyone found using same will be expelled.

Not unlike prison rules, I thought, although having been in prison I knew there was violence. I also knew that any amount of alcohol, drugs, and chemicals were available inside. No, there was something different about this place. It was situated about eight miles outside Dublin city centre, in a suburb called Coolmine, hence the name Coolmine Lodge. And it was exactly that, a lodge, the former gatehouse to a larger estate that had long since fallen into ruin. It was surrounded by trees and fronted by a 500 yard driveway, which led to the highly polished foyer where the bench was situated.

***

I had been sitting there for two hours, listening and sneaking the odd look around, but nothing seemed to be happening that would bring me closer to getting off the bench. I had been told I would have an interview; I found this strange as I'd already been interviewed and I wasn't applying for a job. I wanted treatment for my illness; drug addiction. You don't have an interview before you go into hospital. If you're sick, you're admitted.

My head was full of questions: What kind of an interview? Who would interview me? Why had I been interviewed earlier that day in Jervis Street hospital? What did they want to know?

Three hours sitting there like a fucking dunce. I turned once to ask someone for a drink of water and was told to turn my face back to the wall by this bloke I recognised. He was a pompous little prick from one of the wealthy south coast towns of Dublin, one of those posh junkies from out that way who used to be scared shitless of the likes of me and my mate whenever we'd bump into him in some dingy house or on the street. You could see the nervous tension in his face every time you saw him out looking to score, and you knew he was afraid of the very people he was looking for—dealers and other junkies who would send him running a mile if they said so much as 'Boo' to him. And now, here he was, acting like a Sergeant Major, the little shithead.

I'm getting the fuck out of here, I thought to myself. *I won't put up with this shit from the likes of him or anybody else. How much longer do they expect me to wait? Three and a half hours I'm here now.* I had my last turn-on just before I went to Jervis Street and I was beginning to unravel; I was going to have to leave soon and get a hit.

I was wondering where I could hook up with *Jodie* and the others I had left behind, when I was told to get off the bench and stand against the wall in the large reception room. Finally, something was happening.

There were eight chairs in front of me, and after about ten minutes they were filled by eight people, some of whom I knew from outside, but not a smile or a hint of recognition came from any of them. I'd seen them reach the same depths I had, walking the same streets looking for the same fix, and now here they were, staring at me, judging me.

'Sit down,' I was told by this girl. She went on to introduce the rest of the people, one of whom I already knew because he had brought me from Jervis Street.

'Why are you here?' she began.

'I want to stop taking dope,' I said.

'When did you have your last turn-on?' someone asked.

'About ten hours ago,' I lied.

'Are you stoned now?'

'No, it's worn off.'

'Then you're off dope,' another said, 'so, what's the problem?'

'I want to stay off.'

'Aha,' a chorus of exclamations echoed around the room. 'So what are you going to do about it?' someone else asked.

It was like being in the Bridewell Garda Station, being questioned by eight coppers instead of two.

'I don't know, I've given up before but I can't stay off it.'

'Aha,' again in chorus. 'What are you then?' someone else asked.

'A junkie,' I replied.

'And what are we?'

'You're all junkies too,' I said, as I looked at the familiar faces, and presumed the rest were there for the same reason.

'Ha ha,' they all laughed in unison, 'we're not junkies, we're ex-junkies. Would you like to be an ex-junkie?'

'Yes,' I replied humbly.

'Are you willing to do whatever it takes to become an ex-junkie?'

'Yes,' once again.

Then somebody asked, 'What would you do if you were in a big city, where you'd never been before, and you wanted to find somewhere?'

'I'd ask somebody the way,' I stated.

'What would you be asking for in one word?'

I had to think about that one for a minute.

'Directions,' I said finally.

'Would you be willing to follow directions from any of us, if it would help you become an ex-addict?'

'Yeah,' I said lightly and reluctantly; I was still thinking of *Jodie* and a nice turn-on, just a bus ride away.

'We can't hear you,' they all said in unison.

'Yes,' I said, louder this time, beginning to feel more and more trapped. I hadn't felt so trapped since my first day in training as an encyclopaedia salesman, when the manager was giving us the sales pitch and there was no way of saying no; trapped by my own answers. *Why was I answering all the time?* If I was in the Bridewell, being questioned by two coppers, I wouldn't answer at all, as it only leads to worse shit.

I had learned that when I was 16; the first time I was busted. I had a friend in the Special Branch, and he was going to square it all away, but only in exchange for information. I went around to his house at lunchtime. I was dressed really smartly and, in order to look innocent, I'd removed the earring from my ear, which I'd been wearing for a few months. I'd taken it out for my ma's sake so it wouldn't affect my chances of getting off with the charges against me.

The first thing he asked me was if I wore an earring. It was a big deal in 1968. 'No,' I lied. I'd been an altar boy with his son, and had drunk with him at an engagement party, so I knew him well and had spoken to him many times about anything and everything, but I clammed up then, and I've never opened up to a copper since.

Yet here I was answering every question being thrown at me by the 'ex-junkies'.

'Would you be willing to take directions from anyone in this room?' the guy who brought me from Jervis Street asked, waking me from my daydream.

'Yeah,' I replied, reluctantly.

'We can't hear you,' they said in unison.

'Yeah,' I said louder, feeling a bit pissed off with their attitude.

'If *Breda* told you to scrub the ceiling with a toothbrush, would you do it?' he continued, in his thick Belfast accent.

'Yeah,' I replied once again. I was feeling more and more trapped. Just like when the sales pitch had ended with, 'Any questions?'

I had a question all right: *How the fuck do I get out of here?* I felt like I was being led into a trap.

'You are on a ship,' one of the guys took the lead—it was like they'd rehearsed it—'there's a party going on, everyone is drinking and smoking. You get up to go to the toilet and you fall overboard. The water is cold, the ship is pulling away, you're not a good swimmer, the ship is pulling further away, you're about to go under, what would you do?'

'I'd swim after it.'

They all laughed heartily. I felt like punching somebody, wiping the smug grins off their faces with a few thumps, but I could see where they were going with this.

'What would you do?' another piped up.

I replied meekly, 'I suppose I'd ask for help.'

More titters. 'You'd *ask* for help? The boat is pulling further and further away, you're going under for the third time, what would you do?'

I was feeling really small now, and getting angry, losing my cool. The dope was wearing off and I wanted to split so badly. This wasn't what I thought it would be. This wasn't funny.

'I'd scream for help,' I said, a little louder this time.

'Okay, that's what we want you to do now. Stand up, push your chair aside and shout for help.'

I stood up and pushed my chair aside, but I couldn't do it. I was dumbfounded. I couldn't believe I was doing this. I felt so fucking stupid, standing there being watched by this group who had a question for every answer and who now wanted me to embarrass myself for their entertainment. This was worse than being in court. I couldn't shout for help, not in front of all these people. I tried, I opened my mouth ... *I can't do this* ... Two ... three... four ... five ... ten minutes ... I couldn't do it. I couldn't shout for help, not there, not then, not ever, and not in front of those pricks. No fucking way.

'Go back out and sit on the bench,' one of the guys said dismissively. They all looked kind of disappointed, as if I'd ruined their show.

'Think about why you're here. We have all the time in the world, but you may not have.'

I walked out into the foyer and the first thing that came into my head was that I wanted to walk straight out the door. But I couldn't. Something held me back. I sat back down on the bench.

CHAPTER 2

Help? I needed help, me bollix! I needed a fucking turn-on, or even my bus fare back into town to find *Jodie*, before she went to work for *Mark* or *Bob*. *Those fuckers had no morals at all*, I thought to myself. They once broke into their local church, a few years back, to steal some speakers for a band, and ended up rearranging a body that was lying in the morgue. When the family came to the oratory the next day, the recently deceased was sitting up in the coffin, giving them the finger.

They had no morals; either of them. They'd have *Jodie* working for them in a heartbeat. They couldn't give a bollix about me or the fact that she was my bird.

Help? I needed help a few weeks before that, when it all started to unravel. I'd just dipped some tourist in a pub on Baggot Street, and had relieved them of $2,000 in American Express traveller's cheques. Normally, I would have cashed them all myself, as forgery was one of my fortes, but I'd been busted a few weeks earlier and had a load of outstanding charges, and was out on bail. I knew that if I was nicked again I'd be remanded in custody and, with the kind of habit

22

I had, that was the last thing I needed. There was no way I would be able to stand a stretch in jail, because this time no amount of romantic kisses from *Jodie* at visiting time would be able to supply me with the amount of hard drugs I was going through every day.

It was a bit of a pity really, as I liked doing Amex cheques. It made me feel better, as the victim always got their money back when they reported them stolen, so everyone made out OK except American Express, and they could afford to lose a couple of grand every now and then.

When I lived in London years before, back when I first got into the gear and we had a few quid, we used to buy traveller's cheques and one of us would sign them with the simplest of signatures. Within an hour we'd have cashed them all in, while the 'victim' was reporting them stolen and starting the procedure to have them replaced. It was simple back then—an easy way to double your money.

I couldn't afford to mess about with this lot of cheques though: that's why I was glad I bumped into *Martin*. He had offered to give me 20% of the face value. I had met him in a pub in Aungier Street. He said he didn't have enough money on him, and that he'd have to go back to his gaff in Fatima Mansions to get it. This suited me fine, as I knew about ten different people there I could score from, and even though the Concerned Parents Against Drugs action group were making life difficult for the dealers and the junkies in the area, it was still like the Golden Triangle of Dublin.

It wasn't always like that. When they first built Fatima Mansions the place was considered a major step up from the tenements they replaced. There used to be a community there, but times changed. Jobs went, and so did anybody who could, leaving behind the poorest of the poor. Boarded up flats and dimly lit stairwells gave the dealers and junkies endless places to ply their trade and get a fix, without fear of being caught by gardaí or concerned neighbours. The Concerned Parents could only watch so many places, and there were always new hide-outs to be found as more and more people abandoned the place to its fate.

The dealers ruled the roost, and were supported by a dedicated army of customers, working together in a sort of conspiracy-fuelled belief that the authorities, including the law, were the enemy. The Mansions were clearly for second-class citizens, or so the residents felt, so the authorities were always paradoxically criticised for the lack of services they provided. Law-abiding residents were usually too afraid to act, or even speak out against the tide of addiction that swept over the place. It had gotten so bad that children, with little else to do, turned into runners and lookouts for the main guys, and more often than not, you only had to stand around for a while before some kid would come up and ask if you were looking for drugs.

I'd have no problem scoring as soon as I had the poke. £200 would get me about a gram, which would get me through that night and leave me with a nice turn-on for the morning, and a few quid left over so I could go out stroking again with my old *hors d'œuvre* in good shape. There was nothing worse than looking for a few quid without any gear inside you. It showed in your face, and in your gait. You looked strung out, struggling, desperate, as you walked the streets, looking for a half-chance to grab a handbag or a jacket. You might as well wave a flag for the Gardaí.

We headed off to the flats after finishing our pints, *Martin* in front leading the way, even though I knew exactly where we were going. I had made this journey so many times, down the same old streets, past the same shops and buildings and landmarks, each one telling you that you were that little bit closer to your destination, and that bit closer to a fix.

We kept our heads down once we got to the flat complex, and made our way quickly up the concrete stairs and down the darkened hallway to *Martin*'s. Even though there was little chance of being stopped, we didn't want to take the risk, and I just stayed focused on getting to his place, already looking forward to the buzz, imagining that rush as the needle hits a vein and empties into an arm, or foot, or wherever a vein could be found that hadn't yet collapsed.

Martin suddenly stopped at one of the doors along a dreary hallway. I assumed it was his gaff as he let himself in with a key. It was a pretty nice crib, considering the neighbourhood, and *Martin* told me to make myself comfortable.

He switched on the TV and put the kettle on, and then he asked for the 'chicken necks', as he had to go somewhere else to collect the bread. As soon as he said that, my antennas told me there was something dodgy going on. Normally I wouldn't turn the collateral over to anybody without having the poke in my hand, and especially not to a fence who was strung out.

I mulled it over quickly in my head. I'd known *Martin* a long time; since we were both 16. He was pretty famous in the town then. He was pretty heavy, too, and well-respected for that; definitely not one to be fucked with, even during the period when he was into Guru Maharaji and had 'seen the light' and 'had the Knowledge'.

I respected him for something else, too. A few years earlier we had been stroking a chemist out near Rathfarnham, as there was no gear to be had anywhere. It was 1974 and, back then, importing drugs wasn't as organised as it is now; so, in desperate times, robbing a chemist was one of the only options available. Anyway, we managed to get into this particular chemist, but while we were inside and just opening the DDA cabinet, which held the banned substances, we were bubbled by a passer-by. We managed to get out with the contents of the drug cabinet, which wasn't a lot, and we split to opposite sides of the road, trying to look as innocent as possible. I had really long hair back then and I had stuffed it all inside the jacket I was wearing so it would look short. *Martin* was on the far side of the road, ahead of me, facing the traffic coming from Rathfarnham; and sure enough, within a couple of minutes, a Garda squad car came racing up the road and pulled up beside him. As I drew level with them on the opposite side, they were just putting him into the car, but fair play to him he didn't grass me up and he ended up doing six months. I had decided to give up the gear after that and stayed clean for four and a half years, until this time around. Now fate had let our paths cross again in similar desperate circumstances. I decided to trust him and give him the kites.

He headed off to do the business and I sat back to watch the telly, expecting him to be no longer than half an hour. A half hour turned into an hour, then into two hours. I was starting to get a bit edgy. I felt my initial instincts had been right and I'd been wrong to trust him, and I was really beginning to feel sick now. It had been hours since I'd had a turn-on and I really wanted to believe that he'd be back any minute, but deep down I knew he wouldn't. I had tried to call *Jodie* to see if she had made any money, but she wasn't home, so I really had no alternative but to wait. I was broke and feeling sicker by the minute.

Around midnight, there was a knock at the door; *Martin* had been gone about three hours at this stage and I was sure it was him. I rushed to open it but I was disappointed. Instead of *Martin* there was this guy called *Stevo*. I didn't know him very well but I knew by reputation that he was a heavy. His family controlled the biggest toss school in Dublin, which meant they controlled most of the illegal gambling in the city. They had been doing that for years and had fought off any pretenders to their throne. I also knew that one of his brothers had done a long stretch for attempted murder: he had blasted some bouncer in a cabaret joint with a shotgun because he wouldn't let him in wearing jeans.

As soon as I opened the door, he pushed me into the hallway. 'Where the fuck is *Gaz*?' he asked.

'*Who* the fuck is *Gaz*?' I answered.

'*Gaz* who owns this gaff,' he said. 'Now stop fucking around and tell me where he is.'

I was scared shitless and totally confused. I had come here with *Martin* and was sure it was his place, and now I had this pissed-off gorilla telling me it was someone else's, and demanding to know where this other guy was. I told him really quickly how I had come to be there and that I had no idea who *Gaz* was. *Stevo* knew *Martin* because they were from the same area. He seemed to believe me, and after a few minutes scratching his head, he left.

Relieved, I went back inside and called *Jodie* again. I really didn't want to hang around anymore. Fuck *Martin* and the money; he could pay me later. But I still needed to score. *Jodie* was home, but only had about £30 and as there was no point in going down to her place in Rathmines, where I'd never be able to score at this hour of the morning, so I told her to jump into a taxi and come up to me.

She arrived about half an hour later and, after paying the fare, she had about £25 left; enough for two packs of street shit—just a tiddle to keep me going until I could find someone with gear for sale at this hour of the morning. The only possibility was to find some kids hanging round the stairwells here or up the road in Dolphin House or St Theresa's Gardens—another pair of ironic names for communities that had turned into kips, famous only for the disproportionate numbers of junkies and pushers that inhabited them.

It might sound strange that I was going out looking for kids selling heroin on the stairwells of flats in the middle of the night, but this just shows you how bad Fatima Mansions was back then. More often than not, you would find what you were looking for. This time though, I was out of luck. There was nobody around.

After an hour and a half of looking in vain, I gave up the ghost and headed back to *Martin*'s, where I had left *Jodie* to mind the fort. I was hoping against hope that he might have materialised in the meantime.

I was back in the gaff about half an hour—no *Martin* of course—and was sweating it out, when there was another knock. At this stage I was feeling really sick and wishing it was him, but no such luck. It was *Stevo* again, with another guy I knew, called *Shammy*. This was a problem. There was no love lost between me and *Shammy*, as I used to share an apartment with his sister and her friend, and every time he came to visit there was always tension there.

This time *Stevo* didn't fuck around. He pushed me through the hallway and down onto the couch, screaming, 'Where the fuck is *Gaz*?'

I was in no fit state to go through the whole thing again, so I just sat there wondering who the hell *Gaz* was.

Then he went out into the kitchen and grabbed a carving knife. He made a point of holding it up and showing it to me, looking at the long, jagged blade, then down at me, as if he was imagining where he was going to make his first incision.

At this point *Jodie* threw a wobbler, crying and screaming at him to leave me alone. *Stevo* told her to shut the fuck up or he'd stab me there and then, so she quietened down a little, whimpering a little as she looked from *Stevo* to me.

He grabbed me off the couch and sat me down on a kitchen chair, stabbing the knife into my thigh with just enough pressure to go through my trousers and pierce the skin. I let out a short roar of pain as he put pressure on the blade, letting me feel the sharp pain of its point digging into my leg and the panic well inside me as I saw the blood seep out of the wound and onto my jeans. He looked me in the eyes then, telling me he'd put it right through my leg if I didn't tell him where *Gaz* was.

I was scared shitless. It was a total nightmare. I didn't have a clue where he was or even who he was or what he'd done, and I told *Stevo* so in no uncertain terms, while still trying to keep my cool. But it was hard to keep my cool with a carving knife stuck in my leg and one of Dublin's most dangerous hoods standing over me threatening to cut off my limbs.

I repeated it again; I didn't know who *Gaz* was.

This wasn't helping. He was getting more and more aggravated.

'Well, what the fuck are you and your bird doing in his gaff, then? Are you trying to tell me he left two strangers here with his TV, stereo, video and guitar?'

And with that he picked up the guitar and smashed it over my head. Thanks be to Jaysus it was an acoustic.

I was stunned, and with the guitar dangling around my neck and the pressure of the knife getting worse, I started pleading with him to believe me; *Jodie* was bawling her eyes out at this stage and adding to the hysterical atmosphere, and *Shammy*, the prick, was urging *Stevo* not to believe me, saying I was a lying cunt. There was no alternative but to get him to believe me, otherwise I'd be needing heroin pretty soon for genuine, pain-killing reasons.

The flat was on the third floor and escaping wasn't really a viable alternative, as there were only two ways out; the window or the door, and the thought of jumping from three flights up was worse than the thought of being stabbed. I had managed it once in London, from the second floor onto a shed, but here it would be suicide. I knew, too, that any attempt to make a run for it would only make things worse and, even if I managed to get by him and *Shammy*, I didn't know who was waiting down in the car. I was trying to think and talk and beg all at the same time.

I had been in a similar situation in the past in London, and I'd managed to just talk my way out it, but that had been easier, as the guy with the knife at my kidneys back then had just been a pissed off hippie I'd ripped off with some homemade Pakistani black hash.

This situation was totally different, because the guy holding the knife was a member of one of the heaviest families in Dublin and was well capable of using it. I was really scared and trying my best not to show it. I was begging him to go find *Martin*, who could verify my story, when *Jodie*, who they hadn't been paying much attention to, opened the window and threatened to jump out if he didn't leave me alone. She was screaming at the top of her voice that I didn't know *Gaz* and that she'd have the gardaí there within minutes with her little stunt if they didn't stop.

I think *Stevo* finally realised that, under the circumstances, if I had known where *Gaz* was, I would have told him already. And with that he fucked off, storming out the door with a disappointed-looking *Shammy* in tow. I tore the guitar from around my neck, grabbed *Jodie* down from the window, and we went out on to the balcony to watch them driving away. My heart rate slowed a little as I realised the drama was over, and told my shattered nerves that it would all be OK soon. I knew they wouldn't be back again as it was getting bright, and I decided I was going to hang around to get a turn-on. There wasn't a better place to be for that than Fatima Mansions.

I felt like the third secret had just been revealed. I had honestly felt like I was going to die, to have my wasted life ended by an angry thug in a run-down flat complex in Dublin, but I had been spared. I was sweating and shivering and had terrible cramps though. *Jodie* wanted to take me into bed, happy now that I'd been spared. I wanted to thank her for saving me by giving her all the love she'd been deprived of since birth, but she didn't understand I couldn't unless I was stoned; she'd have to wait until I was, for my full gratitude.

Martin never came back. I hope he got nicked, the little bollix, he'd nearly gotten me killed.

I lay down on the couch in the foetal position as my stomach was in bits. *Jodie* sat beside me, mopping the sweat from my brow. This is what made her happy; mothering me. I was thinking to myself: *What a cliché: the brasser with a heart of gold taking care of her sick boyfriend in his hour of need.* I knew she wanted to be appreciated, to be told how beautiful she was, to hear how much I loved her, wanted her, and needed her. But right at that moment I just felt like telling her to fuck off and leave me alone in my misery.

I didn't, of course, because I knew I'd need her earning power later on, so I just let her continue to mother me until daylight. She was happy 'cos I was the exception to all the men she knew. I didn't want to fuck her, even for free.

We stayed there like that for a few more hours until I got myself together enough to go out looking for some gear. With my leg fixed up with a makeshift bandage, and a bit of a headache from the guitar that had been broken over it, my search began again; business as usual.

I managed to score a couple of packs of heroin in the block across the road. As it wasn't an awful lot, I knew I had to get a mainline hit. I went back across to the flat, by now knowing well that *Martin* wouldn't be back, and got everything I needed together. I cooked it up on a spoon and sucked it into the syringe, not bothering to filter out any of the shit that might be in it for fear of losing any of its potency and, with the help of a mirror, guided the needle up to my neck to get a nice hit in my jugular.

It hit me in a matter of seconds; the sensation of absolute bliss flowing through me like a rush of ecstasy, the euphoria spreading all the way through my body. I felt my arms and legs go heavy, and my eyes roll back in my head, and it was as if I was suddenly caught in the eye of a hurricane— all around me was chaos, but I was calm and at peace and unaffected. Everything was scrambled; I couldn't see, and sounds came to me like dull and muffled noises. It was what I needed. But it didn't last. It never did. After the initial rush, I managed to keep it together long enough to realise that we had to go. I'd gotten what I came here for, albeit by other means, and had risked my life in the process, but I didn't care. It was time to get back out there and do it all over again.

**

With my nerves in order, the sweating and the stomach cramps gone, we were getting ready to leave the gaff in search of more poke when there was another knock at the door.

'Who is it?' I shouted.

'It's me, *Podge*,' came the reply.

Thanks be to Jaysus, someone I knew. I opened the door.

'What the fuck are you doing here? Where's *Gaz*?' he said.

Oh no. Not again, I thought to myself. I knew *Podge* though, and I knew I wouldn't have to go through the same shit with him, even if he was looking for *Gaz* for the same reason as *Stevo*.

Podge was from the flats nearby and his family was just as big and just as heavy as *Stevo*'s. He had lots of brothers and sisters, plus sons, daughters, aunts, uncles, nieces, and nephews, and they all lived in or around the fairly rough parts of Dublin's working class south side. A lot of them did the security in the pubs and clubs of Dublin. *Podge* himself was older than me by a good few years. He was at least 40 and he himself had been a bouncer. He had also been a very successful fence before getting into the drug business, like most of the hoods in Dublin at the end of the 1970s.

He had invested some of his ill-gotten gains into importing a couple of kilos of smack, and had started out as a dealer. I'd been one of his best customers and he always cut me a good deal, as his wife and kids liked me. I always brought them little presents when I went up to score— nothing like a bit of charm to smooth the way to a good deal.

However, he had made the mistake of having the odd snort himself, and eventually became his own best customer. His star began to fade and soon he was out hustling like the rest of us. He lost a lot of respect, too, within his own family, who viewed junkies on a level just above perverts.

As he slithered down from the pinnacle of success, he hooked up with me doing the chequebooks. Every book with a cheque card that was stolen made its way to him. The cheque card guaranteed the cheque for up to £50, as long as the signature jived. I was a pretty good forger and could copy a signature after a couple of minutes of practice, but we had discovered an even better way of guaranteeing the cash. We just dipped the card in brake fluid and after a couple of minutes the original signature would come off. Once the card had dried off sufficiently, I just had to write the name in my own writing. The signature always matched. I got the job of kiting the cheques, as I had a respectable image.

I got to know *Podge* really well during this time. He'd collect me every morning with his collection of stolen books and cards and drive me around all the supermarkets. We never tried to cash them in banks, as they'd have been reported stolen, so we'd just drive to all the suburban supermarkets and sometimes down the country.

It was really easy. I wouldn't bother going shopping for groceries. I'd just go to the off license concession, which had separate tills, and buy a naggin of vodka for £8, write a cheque for £50, which was guaranteed with the card, and walk out the door with a drop of the cratur and 42 smackers for the gear.

We'd hit about four or five in the morning, after a small turn-on to start us off, so he could drive and I wouldn't look too stoned. We'd get stoned back in his gaff during the holy hour, from 2.30pm to 3.30pm, when the off licenses had to close, the same as the pubs, having hit all the salubrious shopping centres and bigger supermarkets; Stillorgan, Dundrum, Rathfarnham, Dun Laoghaire and so on. It was regular as clockwork and almost like having a normal job, with Sunday being the day of rest, when all the supermarkets were closed.

During the holy hour, *Podge*'s wife would make us dinner while he and I were in the jacks cranking up. By the time his kids came home from school, we'd be goofing off in the armchairs watching *Blue Peter* or something similar. *Podge* would be full of love for the god-forbids, the kind of love only a father totally at peace with himself could give. I bet his kids liked him much better when he was on smack than when he'd been a bouncer, as he'd been an aggressive cunt back then. He really trusted me too, 'cos when I finally got nicked I didn't grass him up, and he was able to continue his business with some other poor fucker doing the kites. I should have given the Amex cheques to him and not *Martin*. Hindsight is 20/20 …

Anyway, having asked after *Gaz*'s whereabouts and having been told I didn't know where he was, he said, 'You look rough, do you fancy a turn-on?'

'Is the Pope a Catholic?' I replied.

'Then lets get out of here,' he said.

We jumped into his car and made our way down to the 'shooting gallery' in Marrowbone Lane.

It was an old man's gaff, a pensioner entrepreneur, who made the money for his few pints by renting out his gaff to all the local junkies, so they could have a turn-on in peace. *Podge* and I always gave him a couple of naggins of whiskey when we'd been doing the kites and he'd always made us extra welcome. His wife was dead and all his kids had emigrated, so the likes of us were the only company he'd have during the day. The other added advantage was that he was diabetic, which meant there was always a supply of clean syringes, needles and surgical swabs.

The old man was getting more like a doctor every day. He was 75 and he'd finally found his vocation. He didn't give a fuck about getting busted, and why should he at his age? And when there wasn't a lot of smack around, he didn't mind hitting a doctor for a script of opiates like Diconal or Palfium. He was a more believable patient than the rest of us.

On the way over, I told *Podge* what had happened the night before with *Stevo* and *Shammy*. He said he'd fill me in on the whole deal when we were stoned and *Jodie* was gone, so I knew there was a story behind it.

When we got into the old man's gaff, *Podge* took out some beautiful rocks of uncut Chinese heroin. I didn't even bother to find a vein. I just cooked it up and skin-popped it, straight into my leg, so much nicer than a carving knife.

I followed it up with a nice smoke, chasing the dragon on a bit of tinfoil. After the night I'd just been through, it was heaven: peace, serenity and unaided flight, and all this in a Corporation flat in Marrowbone Lane.

Podge was already well out of it and was starting to come back around by the time I regained my senses, and when *Jodie* and the old man were suitably engrossed in conversation, he took me into the kitchen to explain what had been going on and why I had been caught up in it. The more I heard, the more relieved I felt.

Gaz, whose gaff *Martin* had brought me to, had been sent by *Stevo* to Amsterdam to pick up some scag; altogether £30,000 worth. It was *Stevo*'s family's first venture into the drug business—they were diversifying.

The run had been a success. *Gaz* delivered the gear to the house he had been told to bring it to, and left. Before he had left for Amsterdam though, he had tipped off *Podge*'s crew about the whole deal. After he had made the drop, *Podge*'s boys, pretending to be cops, busted into the gaff and relieved them of the delivered goods. *Gaz*, figuring that *Stevo* might find out he had crossed them, or even just lash out from frustration, decided to get out of town.

Now I had all the information *Stevo* wanted, but about six hours too late as far as he was concerned. I was fucking blessed he hadn't killed me. Dublin was getting worse than New York, divided up among different families and factions. I had been doing bits and pieces for most of them in the past year, but I didn't want to be caught up in the middle of a feud.

I thanked *Podge* for the turn-on and he gave me a nice bit for later, with the warning not to open my mouth about what he'd told me to anyone. With the promise not to breathe a word, and in a way sorry that he'd ever told me, I made some excuse and told him I had to go. He offered to drop me into town but I declined. I didn't want to be seen in his car again. There was going to be war over this and I had no intention of being stuck in the middle. I told him to stay where he was and enjoy the buzz. Stoned as I was, I realised I had to get as far away from *Podge* as possible.

It was a miracle I hadn't been killed really. Not in the usual way a heroin addict loses their life; an overdose, an infected needle, a bad fix, or even the body just giving up after years of abuse, but still, I'd been in danger because of my addiction. If I hadn't been a junkie, I would never have been in that flat, would never have been attacked like that, and would never have needed to be saved. I needed to get out of this whole scene. I needed to go clean.

CHAPTER 3

I was still sitting there in Coolmine staring at the wall as all those memories came back to me; how I had ended up in that flat, with a knife in my leg and a guitar smashed over my head, just because I was desperate for a fix.

That was the day I saw the light and knew I had to escape the addiction I was a slave to, and even though the next couple of weeks saw me sink back into my habit, in the back of my mind I knew it was something I couldn't keep doing. I physically needed the fix, and emotionally needed the love of *Jodie*, but what I needed more was to escape.

That belief had led me here, to a bench facing a wall, where I had all the time in the world to look back at where I had gone wrong.

***

You can die any second. *Memento Homo quia pulveres et in pulverem reverteris.*

I've always had that idea in my head, and as I got older, for me it meant that I should live every day as if it was my last. The trouble is, the way I was living, each and every day could have been my last.

I wasn't always like that though. I was born Catholic; raised to believe that at any second I could kick the bucket, keel over and die, meet my maker, and at that second I had better be as close to perfection as possible, or have just made a true confession. From the time I was seven, every Saturday after my quick whisper with the priest, I wanted to croak saying my penance or, better still, right after communion on Sunday, while still filled with the body and blood of Jesus—just after that moment when I swallowed the host, still young enough to be an angel floating around in Heaven, guarding all of my favourite people, with my sister Pauline who I'd never met because she died before I was born. She was the only angel in the family up to then.

I'm sure that's what started this obsession with the present—the knowledge that I could die at any second. But after a while, the need to be perfect when I bid adieu seemed to fade.

I've got to get out of this obsession with the present, find a way from the past to the future without stopping here. Fuck me, I'm a grown man. I'm not a kid anymore.

But as I sat there facing the wall, all those memories of childhood, of growing up, of friends and family, came flooding back to me like images projected on the wall, a home movie made up just for me.

***

I was a kid once. I was a good kid. I was born and reared in Drimnagh, which was then one of the outer suburbs of Dublin. Our house was one of the private houses at the top end of Drimnagh; most of the other houses were Corporation houses, and the kids from these houses called ours the posh ones.

I didn't come from a deprived area; it was working class, and I was treated well, so I couldn't blame my addiction on anything like that. Anyway, I have seen enough junkies from rich parts of Dublin to know that sometimes there is a deeper cause behind addiction than where you live.

Ours was a three-bedroom house inside a little cul-de-sac, which in turn was inside a big cul-de-sac with a roundabout in the middle. It was a really safe place to grow up and there were always loads of other kids to play with: you couldn't disappear or get murdered or anything. When I was going out to play, my ma always said, 'Don't go further than the top of the culdy,' and I never did when I was little kid. There was never any need to, because anything you wanted to do could be done right there.

There were nine of us altogether; my da, my ma, my three brothers and my three sisters. I was in the middle, with three older and three younger.

Nine was about the average-sized family in our area. Some families had 15 and even 20. All the houses were the same size, with three bedrooms (although one room was really small and called a box room), one bathroom, a toilet, a kitchen, a living room, a parlour, a hall and stairs. It was pretty crowded, but for some of my mates with bigger families it must have been like living in Piccadilly Circus. Some of them even had to turn their parlours into bedrooms.

Our parlour was the best-kept room in the house. It was the room for special guests and there was a piano in it. We weren't allowed in there much and we called it the sitting room, which was kind of funny as it was very seldom someone sat in there.

Sometimes the house would be really busy when one of my aunties came to visit and brought all her kids. All of my aunties had loads of kids and there was always someone making their Communion or Confirmation.

There was always someone having a baby, including my ma, as there wasn't always seven of us kids. She had three after me and I didn't know about any of them until they were already there.

It went like this; Auntie Lily would come over and make dinner that day—I remember it really well as she didn't know how to fry an egg. There were all gooey bits in the white bits and I couldn't eat it. I didn't understand why my ma was up in bed and we weren't allowed to go and see her.

Later on Nurse McAuliffe, the district nurse, would come over on her bike and they'd be boiling loads of pots of water, and then my older brother or sister was sent to get the doctor, and a couple of hours later someone would come down and say you've got a new brother or sister. As far as I knew, getting a new brother or sister took a few hours. I was in the house for three of them and I never even heard a scream—fucking miraculous it was.

Every family had someone your own age and someone the same age as your brothers and sisters.

All I can remember 'til the age of 12 was playing, and all the games had seasons. Conkers, marbles, stilts, gigs, hurling, football, soccer, street leagues, school leagues, the boys' club, the boxing club, and even helping with the housework was a game.

We had no carpets then, only lino. The polish man with the really loud voice would come around and deliver the polish. 'Pure bee's wax, Mrs B,' he'd say to my ma. Whoever was bad that day had to polish and the good ones could shine, pulling each other around the floors on old jumpers or sliding around in old socks that couldn't be darned anymore. Sometimes we'd have competitions to see who could get the best shine on the window handles with the Brasso, or clean the silverware that my parents got for a wedding present, by 'hawing' on it with your breath and shining it with the cuff of your sleeve.

We weren't rich. My da was a driver for Rowntree Mackintosh and he drove a big red truck with pictures of Rolos, Smarties, Fruit Gums and Pastilles painted on the side. He worked day and night to keep us clothed and fed and once a week he'd bring home bags of factory seconds; Rolos, Smarties, Chocolate Whirls, Aeros and other delights. My sisters used to play make up with the Smarties and we'd fight to get the black Fruit Gums and Pastilles.

Sweets were our currency when I was a kid. We used to keep all the ones we liked and trade the others with our friends for conkers, marbles, for a go on their stilts or their roller skates. We didn't have everything but we had access to everything, and whichever game was in season, we had the benchmark currency: Sweets, and loads of them.

My da was great, even though he had to work a lot. He'd leave on Mondays to do his deliveries and come back late on Wednesdays. We'd all be in bed waiting for him, pretending to be asleep. I used to share a bed with my younger brother Joey, and we never let each other go to sleep on Wednesdays. Normally when I couldn't sleep, I used to send him out to flush the toilet and I'd be asleep before the sound of the cascading water was finished, but on Wednesdays we stayed awake. As soon as we heard the sound of my father's key in the door, we'd run down the stairs just as he was giving my ma a kiss.

'How'ya Jim, your dinner's ready. Get back to bed yis little rascals!' she'd shout at us, but she didn't really mean it.

We'd all pile up around him, trying to get his attention to tell him what'd been happening since he left on Monday and to see what he had brought home. Besides the sweets, there were the papers from Monday, Tuesday and Wednesday, cream cakes and gur cakes and other delights from some little bakery down the country, the latest editions of *Newnes Build-Your-Own-Encyclopedia* for the older ones, and comics; *Victor, Hotspur, Beano, Dandy, Judy* and *Bunty* for the younger ones. We'd have our feast in the dining room while my ma served my da his dinner in the kitchen, so that they could have a private chat about their stuff.

On Thursday morning my da'd go to mass at 7am, down in Mourne Road Church. We only went during the week on the first Friday of every month because if you did that nine times in a row you'd never go to hell. Or so we were told. He'd come home from mass and make us breakfast—nothing fancy on Thursdays, not like Sundays when we had a big fry—just tea and toast, and he'd bring it up on a tray to my ma's bedroom. We'd all jump onto my ma's bed and dip our toast in the tea when she wasn't looking, because that was bad manners. My da'd just drink a quick cup of tea, kiss us all goodbye and go to work. He wouldn't eat anything, because he used to have his sambos later in a lay-by on the

Naas Road or somewhere, after he was loaded and off to do his deliveries again, somewhere down the country. He wouldn't be home again 'til Saturday.

Saturdays were much the same as Thursdays but my da would be home earlier. We'd have been to the flicks with some of our pocket money, sixpence for a savings stamp in the post office for Christmas, and sixpence for the Star or the Apollo for the children's matinee. It was always the same: three in a seat and roars of 'look out behind ye, Batman,' during the folly-uppers, as we called the short features, and Baldy the usher shining his torch, telling us to shut up and move over. After it was over we'd run home for our tea because we knew my da'd be home soon with more goodies.

Sometimes we'd run home if we went to the Star because we'd be getting chased by some of the gangs from Crumlin. They'd all be waiting outside the Candy Corner with stones and rocks. We'd have to sprint across the Drimnagh Road and we'd have to go the long way home by the front of Our Lady's Hospital for Sick Children.

Saturday tea was like a preview of Sunday breakfast, with sausages from Byrne's of Chatham Street, back or streaky rashers from O' Neill's in Crumlin, black and white pudding that one of us would buy when we went into town to pay the rent. That was a really responsible job, going into town on the bus to pay the rent in the rent office in Grafton Street, the nicest street in Dublin, with all the posh shops like Brown Thomas and Switzers.

I went with Christine, my next older sister first, before my ma let me go on my own. Christine used to run past the man who minded the lift in the rent office because she was afraid of him, but when I knew where everything was I could go on my own or bring Joey my younger brother with me to show him the ropes.

I always got the lift up. I didn't care what the lift man looked like. You could see all the ropes and pulleys and everything, and I'd go up and down loads of times. Next stop was the butchers; Byrnes of Chatham Street, another great thrill; sawdust on the floor and you could look down over the wooden fence and watch the butchers chopping up the meat. Sometimes we'd go to Clerys on O'Connell Street, and when you paid they'd put the money into a sort of vacuum thing and it got whooshed away to the cash office and then whooshed all the way back with the receipt and change. When we shopped on the Northside we always got the 22 bus home and I'd be looking over at the GPO and Nelson's Pillar and thinking about the 1916 Rising and how all the heroes had freed us from England, because I was learning about that in school.

After tea on Saturday my ma'd put the roast in the oven for the Sunday dinner. Then she'd get ready and her and Da would go to the cinema and afterwards for a few gargles in the Halfway House or McCann's.

We'd be left at home and whoever was the oldest was the babysitter until an older one came home. When Peter, Liz and Christine went to confession or somewhere else, I'd be in charge. After I put the younger ones to bed I'd go downstairs and get a big knife out of the kitchen and I'd always sit in a corner with my back to the wall so no one could get me from behind. I'd sit like that with the knife so I'd be able to get anyone who came in and they couldn't get me or the little ones upstairs. Even when the older ones came home I wouldn't open the door until they shouted in the letterbox and I knew it was them. Then I'd put the knife back and run upstairs to make sure everyone was all right, checking their breathing before I'd open the door. No one was going to die on my shift.

After they came back they'd send me up to bed but, more often than not, I'd wake up to the sound of the piano and someone singing. Nearly every week my da'd bring a gang back from the pub. A great gang they were too. They could all play an instrument or sing and there'd be a great hooley. We'd all be sitting on the stairs in our pyjamas listening, and eventually when everybody had enough to drink we'd be invited down too, to do our party piece.

It was a great way to get a few bob, as everybody would root in their pockets for change to give us, telling us what great kids we were. My ma'd warn us not to take the money but we always did. They were great parties.

***

When I was about 11 or 12, the Christian Brothers tried to prepare us for Secondary school with a retreat which was held in the school. Three days of prayers and silence, yapping away to beat the band, and smoking behind the bicycle sheds. This was followed by confession with a Monsignor in the school office. No confession box, just me and the Monsignor. I told him my usual sins; the same ones I'd told since my communion: I told lies, I was disobedient, I talked in the church. I always said the same ones to see how the penance would differ.

I supposed the penances would go to the debit side of the indulgences I'd been saving over the years. I knew I wasn't going to hell anyway, as I'd done the nine first Fridays, so I was covered. But then the priest asked, 'Do you ever get stiff?' I wasn't sure I knew what he was talking about. I thought he meant a boner; although he could've meant stiff after football or something.

I said, 'Yeah,' anyway.

Then he asked, 'How often?'

I looked sort of quizzically at him and said, 'I don't really know what you mean father.'

'How often do you get stiff down there?' he asked.

I was thinking now, from the neck down I must have looked puzzled because he explained.

'Down there, between your legs.' He meant a boner. It was easy, but I knew I shouldn't say loads of times so I said, 'A couple of times.'

'When does it happen?' he asked

'When I sit on the big seat on the back of the bus.'

'What do you be thinking about when it happens?'

'Nothing father.'

'That's good. There's nothing wrong with it,' he said. 'That means your mother was a virgin when she got married.'

I was glad to hear that. I knew Our Blessed Lady was a virgin when she had Jesus and now I knew my ma was a virgin when she got married. I felt like I understood the relationship, and was glad to be part of the mystery.

I didn't tell him that I got one when I was playing doctors and nurses, or even when we were playing doctors and doctors in the ferns behind Porter's field in Portrane when we were little kids. The other kids' Mammies must have been virgins too, 'cos they all had a boner. That was what I learned on my last retreat, preparing me for Secondary school—the relationship between virgins and boners. I left that confession box enlightened.

The metamorphosis was really quick. One year I was 14, good at school, playing for the school hurling and football teams in Croke Park, running cross-country, and working during the school holidays as a messenger boy in Brown Thomas. Brendan worked next door in Brown and Nolan; he was a little bit older than me and was playing in the Gingermen, a ballad group, with John from our cul-de-sac. He was great craic and we had great times in the lane behind the shops when there were no messages to be delivered.

Within 18 months I was getting stoned, stealing, getting arrested, and running away. What the fuck had happened to me?

**

From the time I was 15 going on 16, I wanted to risk death every day. I didn't want to die; just dice with death. I was too old to be an angel and no more full of the host, no more striving for perfection, no more confession, no more mass, just a daily dice with death the leveller.

It was an adventure a day; a long way from 18 months earlier, when me and my mate used to spend the afternoons counting cars at the end of the newly finished dual carriageway that they'd built out of the Long Mile Road. There was nothing better to do then, except maybe hanging round in the hallway of the snooker hall where we used to look through the window at the sharks because we were too young to go in to this 'den of iniquity' as my ma used to call it.

CHAPTER 4

*S*hit, *that's going back a long time; the more recent past is more relevant to my present situation.*

There was no way out of my problems with the law unless I could convince some judge that I was making a serious shot at rehabilitation. I'd been sent forward for trial to the Circuit Court and I was sure to be found guilty, and considering the amount of stuff I'd been involved in, and the people I knew and hung around with, I was in for a long stretch. If the cops brought up how I'd known one of the biggest drug dealers in Dublin they would definitely throw the book at me. It wasn't as if I was part of the organisation; one of them just let me stay with them because I had nowhere else back then. But I'd been there when they busted it a few times, and one and one makes more than two in their eyes.

That's how I had been busted in the first place. They were watching everything I was doing. Because I'd been into the gear before, then gave it up, then went back onto it, I think they saw me as some kind of consultant for the new hoods.

My luck had been running out anyway. It was only a couple of weeks since I'd been in the wrong place at the wrong time on that night in Fatima Mansions, caught up in a dispute between two rival mobs, which could have been the end of me.

Think. Think, you fucking eejit. Don't get up off this bench without thinking. Think about the future.

How could I think about the future? It hasn't fucking happened yet. How the fuck could I think about it? The idea disgusted me. What could it possibly bring? Wife, kids, retirement … it hasn't happened yet, but I know it's coming.

What the fuck ever happened in the future? You can't live in the future; you can only live now, right fucking now. The future is like something you're promised so you can't enjoy the present.

Now is awesome, it's an experience that can't be transcended, it's creation, it's pure, without afterthought—happening right fucking now.

I was driving myself crazy with this internal dialogue. *Why didn't someone come along and do something? How long did I have to sit there staring at the wall?*

I started asking myself some serious questions, and I realised I did want to get out of the life I was stuck in. I no longer wanted to find myself hanging around the very worst parts of Dublin, looking for a fix from some guy I wouldn't want to ever meet in any other circumstances, or wake up slumped in some piss-stained laneway with a belt tied around my arm and a used syringe hanging limply from whatever vein I managed to locate and pierce that day. But I didn't want to give up all the best bits of that life.

Being stoned—who'd want to give it up? Who the fuck knows what it's like to dip a handbag with a few grand in it in Dublin and just head for some fancy hotel, or in Kensington

High Street, check into the Inn on the Park on Hyde Park corner, and shoot up the best scag in the most luxurious surroundings, be totally satisfied, flying aimlessly in orbit, unfettered by the future, enveloped in the present. No consequences, no decisions, no responsibility, no worries, just absolute peace with a beating heart and happiness coursing through your veins—in the RIGHT NOW. Loads of people never have the chance to enjoy now; like my ma.

I would have loved to turn her on, just say forget about everything, stop worrying, just try this, everything will be all right. But then, of course I wouldn't, and nor would she. She lived in the past after my da died, and worked for the future, for her children, and never got free from the responsibilities she had. I got my freedom because my da died. That's one way of looking at it. In other ways, I gave it all away by throwing my future aside and getting seriously into drugs. Because of this, my ma got a sentence, and I became her torturer.

**

1968 was a really weird year for me. My da got sick on Christmas Eve in 1967. He was supposed to go to work that day, as it was a really busy time for delivering sweets, so he must have been especially sick to take a day off. He had a headache and he'd vomited that morning. My ma thought it was because he'd had a few pints the night before with his brother and a few of his mates from work, and maybe he'd drunk a bad one.

We were delighted he was home though; it was so unusual on a working day. As a kid I only remember him being home during the week a few years earlier when he'd been recovering from a stroke.

I'd been distancing myself from my da in the last couple of years. I didn't need his approval or attention like I used to, and he didn't really like my ideas or my new mates, and stuff like that began to cause us to drift apart. I didn't want to go to the children's mass anymore or to the beach with the rest of the family on Sundays. I'd enjoyed the holiday in Butlins holiday camp that year though; it had brought us closer together. But I still didn't like it when he brought attention to me for the wrong reasons, like when he prayed out loud at mass like you're supposed to or sang the hymns with the choir.

Since I was 13 he'd acquired this ability to make me look and feel like a gilly when I was in his company. I didn't want people to think I was religious like him or that I still went on picnics, but now it was Christmas and he was home and I had all the good old family feelings again. None of my mates were around and I wouldn't look like a fool, no matter what he did. He was my da, it was Christmas, and he was home.

He was sick now. Like years before after he'd had the stroke, he'd been home for weeks and he didn't need money or anything as the men at work had done a collection every week, and his mate Andy would come every Thursday to see him and give my ma the money from the sick fund. He was able to come and watch us playing football and hurling and soccer.

He'd played for Saint James' Gate; one of the best teams in Ireland at the time. If he hadn't had to work all the time, he probably would have been brilliant and played for Manchester United, like Tony Dunne who lived around the corner on Kilworth Road. He had injured his knee too, and he had to wear a tight woollen stocking on it.

I remember thinking, when I was eight or nine, *I wish me da was sick all the time so he could be with us every day and he didn't have to work.*

He had loads of mates who'd take care of him and give him money. Not just the ones from work but the ones who were at parties in our house every Saturday night when I was a little kid; garage owners, tailors, actors, musicians, milkmen, newsagents, singers all getting drunk and singing and eating ham sandwiches and slipping us ha'pennies, pennies, thruppenny bits, tanners, shillings and even half crowns. There were thousands of people who'd take care of his wages.

Everybody loved him but no one loved him as much as me.

This Christmas my da was sick again and I'd have time to mend the cracks that had been appearing in our relationship, close the distance that had come between us. It was going to be a great Christmas.

Anne and Johnny were still young enough to believe in Santy. Dave, Liz's boyfriend, would be having Christmas dinner with us, as they were getting married the following July and were going to emigrate to Canada, so it would be their last Christmas with us for a while.

If he was going to be sick long enough, maybe he'd have more time to spend with Anne and Johnny and teach them stuff the way he'd taught me and Joey, the last time he'd been ill, to do all the things he would have loved to be able to do all the time if he didn't have to work, to share himself with them the way he'd shared himself with us.

This Christmas I was going to be a good kid again. My da stayed in bed all day and we brought him up his dinner and his tea. He just picked at the food and he didn't even want a drink. We had bottles of Guinness and Smithwicks and Harp and all kinds of lemonade, like we always did at Christmas, but he had no interest in it; his headache was really bad.

I got really busy helping my ma, getting things ready for Christmas day, plucking the turkey that Paddy our neighbour who was a butcher had slaughtered that morning. We'd had the turkey for weeks after my da had brought it home from some turkey farm down the country. We called it Tessie and had been feeding it and it was a bit sad to see it killed. We had a goose that year too, for the first time, and that was really hard to pluck. There were little feathers everywhere and we all had a go at plucking it.

Finally, late in the evening, everything was ready; turkey, goose, cakes, puddings, ham, mince pies, the whole shebang, but my da didn't get up to go to midnight mass and when we came home I had to get up in the attic to bring down the toys for the younger ones and put them under the Christmas tree.

Christmas Day was great. The kids were delighted with their presents and I pretended to be delighted with mine; a couple of books, a respectable jumper, a shirt and tie. My da was a bit better too. We'd called a doctor for him and he had given him some tablets to help his headache, so he seemed really happy when we went to his room to show him our presents and to give him his. He got up for dinner but went back to bed straight after.

St Stephen's Day, and every day after, was much the same. The doctor would come every morning and examine him, and leave a prescription or whatever was necessary. The holidays went by and we all went back to school or work but my da was still sick and stayed in bed all the time now. I'd be first home at lunchtime and after wolfing down my dinner I'd go up and talk to him.

I knew my ma was really worried, as it had been a couple of weeks now and he showed no sign of getting better, but she acted as normal as possible, especially with the younger ones around. The older ones didn't come home at lunchtime and because I was a teenager, she'd confide in me. But she was confident that everything would be OK as the doctor was coming every day and he was familiar with my da's history. He'd tended to him the last time he got out of hospital.

When I'd talk to my da at lunch time and after school, he'd do his best to be cheerful and when Joey, Anne and Johnny came up to his bedroom, we'd all tell him about school; he loved that, he really believed in education and wanted us all to do our Leaving Certificate, like Peter and Liz, and maybe even go to college.

It was great to have him there, even though he was sick.

During this time I made a conscious decision not to do anything to upset my ma. I wore the right clothes to school, came home on time and generally did all the right things.

One Thursday in the second week in January, I was talking to my ma in the kitchen, just the two of us. She was telling me my da was really bad. I felt like her friend or something. She was really upset and cried a little and I comforted her as best I could, telling her everything would be all right.

We were interrupted by a knock at the door; it was Andy, my da's friend from work, with his sick pay. The three of us were sitting in the living room, having a cup of tea when my da appeared on the stairs. He was screaming in pain, screaming for my ma to help him.

'My head, Mary, my head. The pain is killing me, how could God do this to me?'

We were shocked, and my ma and Andy rushed up the stairs to put him back to bed.

I was shaken by his last few words: 'How could God do this to me?' This was my da, who went to mass and communion every day before he went to work. My da, whose oldest son had studied for the priesthood, who'd never hurt a fly, who worked six days a week, 14 hours a day to keep us clothed and fed, and he was asking my ma how God could do this to him—to me *he* was God, and he was in terrible pain.

When they came downstairs Andy and my ma were both crying, and they decided we should have a second opinion from the Rowntree's doctor who didn't cost anything. My ma gave me the money for the phone call and I called him from the phone box at the top of the road. I told the doctor's secretary what had happened and that it was an emergency, and he arrived within minutes.

He went straight up to my da's room, examined him, took his blood pressure, and within a couple of minutes he came down and said, 'Mrs Byrne, your husband has had a stroke. I'm calling an ambulance and having him removed to hospital.'

The next hour was a total blur. My brother and sisters arrived home from work, the younger ones came in from playing, and all the neighbours in the cul-de-sac stood at their doors with their hands over their mouths in shock, as they watched my da being loaded into the ambulance.

I don't know how I felt then. Peter and Liz went with my ma to the hospital, Christine started to make the dinner, and some of the neighbours came in to ask what had happened.

'My da had a stroke.'

'Oh no, not your … not a stroke … Oh my God …'

My God, my da, my God.

***

We had our tea and said our grace before the meal, as he always did—it had an extra significance now—and began reassuring ourselves that everything would be OK now that my da was in hospital. Sure, didn't he have a stroke before and recover completely? My ma came home a few hours later and said he was sleeping and sent us all to bed.

The next few days were as normal as possible, except my da wasn't in the bedroom, he was in hospital—St Stephens, near the Guinness brewery—and he was in intensive care. My ma could visit any time of the day or night. She took advantage of the liberal visiting hours, setting out first thing in the morning on the number 23 bus as soon as we were all off to work or school. She'd come home in time to prepare our dinner and she'd go back in the afternoon.

About four days after my da'd been taken to hospital, I ran home at dinner time and knocked on the door. There was no answer. I banged hard on the knocker. I was frantic, peeping through the letter box. Finally I saw my ma open the kitchen door. I was relieved but she was dabbing her eyes; she'd been crying and once again I was the only one there to comfort her.

'He'll be all right, Ma,' I said, trying to sound confident. 'He got better the last time, didn't he?'

I'd never seen my ma crying before, though I'd seen my da crying once. He had been accused of breaking a picket during a strike when he'd left his truck back in the yard because he didn't want to leave it out on the street; and as he was explaining to my ma that he hadn't clocked in or claimed overtime or anything. He was crying, and I chose that moment to burst into the kitchen where they were having their little chat. It was a sight I would never forget.

Now my ma was crying and I was the only one there to help her. I wished someone else would come. I felt so inadequate and I didn't know what to do or say. A couple of minutes later Joey, Anne and Johnny arrived home and I was relieved. My ma had stopped crying by that time, but Joey knew there was something wrong. He had good instincts. Anne was ten and Johnny was only eight, so they hadn't got a clue what was going on.

We finished our dinner and went back to school. It was Thursday; exactly a week since my da had gone into hospital. I was unravelling slowly. On Friday night, my Auntie Bridie, who was one of my da's sisters, came over with her husband Paddy. I went out with my mates. I took my sister's bike because mine was broken, and headed up to the snooker hall. On Friday nights, Peter, the old guy who worked there, used to let us in to watch the big pool game on the number one table. We didn't have money to play, even if we'd been allowed, but we had enough for ten Major, a Club Orange, a Crunchie and a single of chips on the way home.

It was great watching the sharks playing, right hand side, left hand side, screwback, and stop; the only way to learn was by watching the experts. It was my first night out with my mates since my da'd been taken ill. I knew my ma was chatting away with Bridie and Paddy and my da was safe in hospital.

I felt really great for the first time in weeks and at about 10.30pm, after knocking around a few balls when the lights were off, we got ready to leave. I was going to buy my chips and be home before midnight, which was the limit, and I wasn't going to break it in the circumstances. When I got out in the hallway my sister's bike was gone. All the other bikes were there but mine was gone.

Who'd want to rob a girl's bike out of the snooker hall? I was sure my mate *Tommo* was messing again like he used to when I'd bring him down to my house and he'd always steal something, like a statue from the parlour, but he insisted it wasn't him.

I was in a heap. How would I explain this to my ma? How could I add this to the problems she already had? I hadn't got permission to take it in the first place.

How could God let this happen? I was beginning to lose faith in him. First of all he was giving my da all this pain and now he'd let Christine's bike get robbed from outside the snooker hall—the den of iniquity—if you were a good player it was the sure sign of a misspent youth.

God was definitely becoming a problem, letting this shit happen. This wasn't just a bike that was stolen, this was Christine's approval machine, her way of showing to the world that she was saving three bob a week on bus fares—one tenth of her wages. It was gone and I hadn't even told anyone I planned to borrow it.

We decided there was nothing we could do and headed towards the chipper to eat our soggy singles drowned in salt and vinegar and maybe get a game of table soccer in the amusement arcade next door with Roberto, if he had no paying customers.

We'd just reached the chipper when my older brother Peter pulled up, brakes screeching, on Christine's Raleigh.

'What are you doing in the snooker hall when your father is dying in hospital?' he shouted—like my da was dying *because* I was in the snooker hall. He grabbed me and pushed me on my way.

'Get home immediately,' he yelled after me.

I'd been trying to be good for weeks, comforting my ma, staying away from my mates, trying not to do anything wrong, and now it was all my fault my da was dying. I was delighted Peter had the bike though. At least that wasn't my fault.

When we got home, my ma gave Peter the keys to my da's car so we could go and visit him. It was almost midnight and I was hoping there was a fault in this reality. It was *too* fucking real. I wanted to change the reality; I wanted to change the fault. It wasn't *my* fault. It wasn't *my* reality.

My emotions had been through the wringer in the last half hour and I didn't know exactly what I was feeling as I drove with Peter to the hospital. There was a kind of silence between us. He was talking to God, saying the rosary. He'd start: 'Hail Mary.' I'd finish: 'Holy Mary.' We'd been communicating like this for years, through intermediaries; we'd never spoken to each other. I couldn't talk to him like an older brother; I couldn't curse in front of him. It was like he'd been kidnapped by the priests and had gone straight from Secondary school to the seminary and stayed there for four or five years, and even though he'd left the priests now and had come home from Spain where he'd been training a couple of years earlier, he was still really religious.

He always had been. Even when I'd started in the Christian Brothers' Primary school and he was in the Secondary, he used to give me a lift to school on the crossbar of his bike. He'd be saying his prayers, the 'morning offering' on our way. He'd pray and I'd say the responses. It was a really weird kind of conversation. If my responses weren't rehearsed I didn't know them. The other thing about Peter was that he'd been brilliant in school and got honours in everything and, as the same teachers were still there when I went, they were always comparing us:

'Seamus, you'll never be as good as your older brother Peadar.'

We were both in the special class for learning things through Irish, but they didn't realise that I didn't want to be as good as him, and kind of made it my goal not to be. It was like having Saint Dominic Savio as an older brother.

I wanted to have an older brother who was crap at school. I wanted an older brother I could talk to, who liked tits, girls, football, drinking, showbands, things I could relate to, a guide through the minefield of adolescence, not someone who prayed to God, Jesus and the Virgin Mary. All I'd ever had were older sisters, who at one point had stopped being older sisters and had become objects of desire, not for me, but for all the guys on the road. They'd say to me, 'Your sister is gorgeous.'

So here I was on my way to the hospital to visit my da who was dying because I had borrowed my sister's bike and went to the snooker hall with my mates on a Friday night. Me and my older brother, who'd talk to God, and who hadn't been there a week earlier to answer the question my da had asked: 'How could God do this to me?'

***

We reached the hospital by the fifth decade of the sorrowful mysteries, parked the car and made our way through the courtyard and under the balustrades of St Stephen's Hospital to the intensive care unit on the first floor. If anyone ever needed intensive care it was my da. He needed to be loved, cherished, nourished, cured, blessed—whatever it took.

He was in an oxygen tent, smoking his finger, sucking on himself to stay alive. He'd become tiny in the week since I'd seen him. I looked at him and understood he had done everything for his family that he possibly could. He had no faults, no weaknesses, he understood his own perfection, he'd realised himself.

I put my hand in his hand and he gripped it in a way that's hard for me to describe. It was strong, stronger than anything I'd ever felt before. He didn't need to talk, he didn't need to hear. As long as he could hold on to me or Peter he could hold on to life, like we could infuse him with ours. We stayed for a couple of hours, just looking and praying and bridging the distance between us with the grip that said it all.

Peter and I drove home in silence. I could tell he was angry. I could feel his intensity and I knew he didn't know how to handle it. I knew he felt the same as me and he had no one to talk to about it except God. I felt really sorry for him.

My ma, Auntie Bridie, uncle Paddy and my older sisters were still awake when we got home.

'How is he?' my ma said.

'The night sister said he was comfortable,' Peter replied.

I went to bed, climbed silently in beside Joey and covered myself up with the blanket and imagined my da was with us and we were all really warm and snug. I wanted to join him in his oxygen tent and keep him warm like he used to keep us warm when he came home on winter nights and threw his big coat over us. I wanted to throw a big heavy Rowntree Mackintosh overcoat over him because he'd looked so cold and I felt guilty for leaving him in the hospital on his own because there was no one there who loved him like we did.

On Sunday morning my ma took us to mass and communion and I think I prayed like I really meant it. When we got home she made breakfast and started to prepare dinner. She hadn't gone into the hospital that morning so she could look after us younger ones. She let Peter, Liz and Christine go and she would go in the afternoon.

When they came home the news was good—my da was much better—he'd spoken to them, and he hadn't spoken for days before that.

He spoke to Liz mostly; as her wedding was coming up in July—the first one in our family—and she and her fiancé Dave had now decided for sure to emigrate to Canada after the deal they were working on to buy a new house had fallen through. My da's motto had always been 'the family that prays together, stays together' and our family had done its fair share of praying over the years. What with masses, rosaries, novenas, retreats, vigils, sodalities, processions, it was hard to envisage that we could ever be apart after all that. And on this Sunday morning my da had sat up and reiterated the point to Liz and he seemed perfectly normal. We were all delighted and we had a really enjoyable dinner. It was like a belated Christmas dinner.

I was especially delighted 'cos now I could really enjoy the afternoon dance at Moulin Rouge, a really cool club in Georges Street, and that day a brilliant band called Skid Row were going to be playing. They were as good as any band coming out of England or America. They were a four piece band led by Brush Shiels on bass, Nollaig Bridgeman on drums, a new guitarist named Gary Moore from Belfast on lead—he was only 15 and used to play with a band called the Interns and was as good as Clapton or Hendrix—and a lead singer called Philip Lynott from Crumlin, near me, who I knew from when he played with the Black Eagles in the Moeran Hall in Walkinstown. He was one of the few black kids around, and skinny, with an afro like Jimi Hendrix.

They didn't just play; they had a whole media extravaganza. I knew the road crew—Frank Murray and Paul Scully from Walkinstown—they were my heroes from when I used to hang out at the snack bar at the Apollo cinema, all long hair and cool clothes. Another mate of theirs, Mousey, used to do the background videos with an old projector on to a canvas background and when Phil sang 'Sky Pilot', the backdrop would show news clips from the Vietnam War. The last guy in the crew was Lasher Delarue, who worked in an electrical shop and made up all the plugs and stuff they needed. I wasn't even going to have to pay in because the DJ was the cousin of one of my mates from school and he got us free passes.

I was feeling great, my da was talking again, and I was just ready to leave when Mrs Hickey, our neighbour from across the culdy, came over to say there was a phone call from the hospital. We didn't have a telephone so we had given their number for emergencies. Peter took the call. It was Christine, who had gone to visit with my ma and Liz. My da had taken a turn for the worse. Peter came back over and told me to get ready to go to the hospital with him. Joey was left in charge of the two younger ones and we set off once again. When we got there, a few other people were there; my uncles Christy, Tom and Jack, my aunties Mabel, Nellie and Hannah. It was a cold January day and throughout the afternoon loads more people arrived; all my da's friends and relatives. We were allowed into his room three and four at a time, and everybody else waited in the corridor, alternatively talking or kneeling down saying the Rosary, my da's favourite prayer.

Every time I looked into his room it reminded me of the crib in the church at Christmas, only now my da was the baby Jesus. He'd shrunk so much he looked like a baby, surrounded by Mary and Joseph, the shepherds and the three wise men. His breaths were getting shorter and the interval between them longer. We had arrived at the hospital at about 2.30pm and despite everyone who was there willing him to live, at 7.20pm, after what seemed like an eternity, he drew his last breath.

I waited for the next one and it didn't come. Everybody cried except the men and my older brother Peter; he was strong. I was weak and I bawled me eyes out until I was empty, then I bawled again. I wasn't a man, I was a teenager, 15 years of age, and I'd just watched some nasty cunt steal my da's last breath.

The only thing left inside me were salty tears, cascading through me—I wished they'd fucking drown me. I wanted to be with my da, he was happiness and he was gone. I was void of happiness. I was fucking angry, and I was fucking sad.

The nurse made us all leave the room while they prepared his body for the morgue, letting the nuns measure him for his burial habit—his last suit. He always looked great in suits, tailor-made by my uncle Paddy. His Rowntree Mackintosh uniform was also made by Paddy because my da had organised the contract for him to make all the suits for Rowntrees. He was always doing things like that; helping people to get on in life. He had also arranged a contract with Rowntree for his friend Davy the mechanic, to service all their trucks in his garage up at the Red Cow on the Naas Road.

Davy had been a mechanic with Ferrari and used to work on the racing driver Fangio's car but he was married now and had come back to Ireland to set himself up in business. My da had helped him get started up.

As we drove home from the hospital in my da's black VW Beetle, with Peter at the wheel, I was thinking about all the cars he had owned over the years since I was a little kid; Vauxhalls, Wolselys, Morrises, Austins. They all looked like gangster cars with running boards, and doors that opened out the wrong way, and indicators that popped out from between the doors. They all needed a starting handle to crank them up and if that didn't work, we'd all have to jump out and push them around the roundabout where we lived.

He bought them all from Bill, who was the salesman in the Red Cow, and I don't think any of them cost more than a tenner. Then one day he came home with the Beetle.

It was fairly new compared to the others and I think he had to pay about £50 for it in instalments, but it was the best deal he ever made because it never broke down. We'd been all around Ireland in it. It reminded me of all the happy times we'd had together, and now here we were going home in it, but he wasn't driving, and he wouldn't be driving it ever again.

I was sitting in the back with my two older sisters holding me. They were crying too, but they were holding me because it seemed like I'd fall apart. I felt so empty, like I could just cave in.

Peter was praying as he was driving, I didn't know who to. For me, there was no one left to pray to, no one left to be good for.

When we got home, a couple of the neighbours were already there in the kitchen, cooking and making sandwiches, preparing for the wake. Joey, Anne, and Johnny were in different neighbours' houses with their friends. My uncles, and aunts, and my da's friends who had been in the hospital had all gone to the pub to help drown their sorrows.

I was sent over to Peter Mac's house to get Joey, so my ma could tell him and the younger ones what had happened. She didn't need to tell Joey, because as soon as he came out of Peter Mac's house, he said to me, 'Daddy's dead isn't he.'

I just nodded my head and put my arm around him on the short walk back to our house. I felt really sorry for him. I'd never been an angel, but up to that time I'd never done anything really bad, just mitching from school, or sneaking cigarettes from the packets they'd leave lying around, or bringing Joey to see *Carry on Cleo* in the Savoy instead of *Mary Poppins* in the Adelphi, just so he could see a bit of tit.

When Anne and Johnny were brought home, my ma took the three of them aside and told them my da had died and gone to heaven. They were all crying, but the younger kids believed he was in heaven. Anne had just made her Confirmation and Johnny, his Communion. I don't know what Joey believed. He was 13, two years younger than me, but some time after the funeral, he showed me this poem that he'd written:

Horizontal
Six feet down
Covered by a ton of ground
Marble headstone
Golden scroll
Your resting place
Your bell has tolled
Your family stand all wet with grief
Your good friends glare
And curse the thief
Who took the ones they laughed and loved with
To go before them to their own relief
Stand up, sigh, shed a tear, walk away.

I knew when I read it he felt the same way as me. God was a thief. That's why Jesus was surrounded by thieves when he was crucified.

***

All sorts of people started arriving back at the house then, carrying bags full of every kind of alcoholic delight. Our

grief was to be forgotten; now it was time for a celebration—
a celebration of my da's life.

The house was packed. There were people everywhere,
in every room, on every step of the stairs. The party got
going in earnest, and it was just like old times.

It reminded me of when I was kid, sitting on the stairs in
my pyjamas, watching the revellers through the banisters;
except now I could join in, and have a drink, and listen to
all the stories about him that I'd never heard before. I heard
how he used to raise canaries when he was single, how he
had an instant family when he got married first. My ma's
two younger single sisters had moved in with them, as they
didn't want to live with their stepmother anymore. There
were other stories about how it was during the war, and how
despite everything, they still managed to have a good time.
I learned more about my da that night than I had when he
was still alive.

Everybody sang a song my da would have loved to hear,
but no one sang his song: 'Old Man River'; no one had that
deep bass voice.

I had a few beers that night too, and sang mine: 'Sunny
Afternoon' by The Kinks. It was the same one I'd sung the
year before, in the talent competition in Butlins Holiday
Camp. He'd been so proud of me, even though I didn't win,
as I was in the adult section: 14 onwards.

The other younger ones: Joey, Anne, and Johnny
did win their sections, and another free weekend for the
family for the finals later on that year in September, just
before Butlins closed for the season. It had been the year
of my parents' 25th wedding anniversary, which had been
celebrated with a great party, and everything was looking
good for the future. The older ones were working, money

was a bit easier, we could afford to go on holidays and not just drive to the beach, and it was even possible now for my da to turn down some of the overtime he had always had to work in order to keep us all alive.

Now we were celebrating his existence. He was everywhere; on everyone's tongue, in everyone's ear, in everyone's teary eyes, in everybody's loving touch, and in everyone's feelings. They were drowning those feelings to unlock the happy memories that everyone associated with him: Jim, JB, Da.

I remember my Auntie Hannah sitting on the stairs beside me, laughing, and crying, and telling me what a great guy he'd been.

I don't know when I got to bed that night, certainly not until the early hours, and the next day when I woke up, I thought I had dreamt it all. I went down stairs, and there were all sorts of people still there, but they weren't singing or drinking anymore. It was really quiet; no radio on. In the kitchen, they were busy dying clothes black, and in the living room they were sewing black diamonds on the sleeves of jackets, in preparation for the funeral. I hadn't dreamt it all; it was for real.

Later that day, the limousines from the undertakers took us to the morgue in the hospital to view the body before they put the lid on the coffin, and I kissed my da's body. He was dressed in a brown habit like a monk, with rosary beads wrapped around his fingers. He looked like a statue, and kissing him was like kissing the feet of the statue of St Anthony in Whitefriar Street church. It was horrible, and I'd never remember him like that, dressed like a monk, and cold as stone.

I'd been to loads of removals of the remains when I was an altar boy; it was always solemn, but I wasn't involved. This was different. All of my mates were at the church, along with teachers, brothers, nuns from the schools, classmates, and colleagues. It was like everyone any of us had ever known was there. After the short ceremony, it was back to the house for more visitors, more drinks; sadness to gaiety to sadness—an emotional merry go round.

After the funeral mass the next morning, the hearse drove by our house for the last time. As we drove down the Crumlin Road in the Austin Princess limousine, towards the graveyard in Mount Jerome, it all seemed so unreal. Watching the people going about their business, I wanted to scream; I wanted to tell them to stop doing what they were doing, did they not know what had happened? My da was dead and they were acting like nothing had happened. I wanted to scream so loud they'd all go deaf, but I didn't, I couldn't. I was on my way to a funeral. I was sad. I didn't scream. I kept the scream inside. I cried instead.

Inside me though, something was hardening. I'd seen what reality brought, and I wanted no part of it. I couldn't go through what I was feeling that day ever again, and if there was a way out of the responsibilities of life, and death, I was ready to sign up. It wasn't long before I found out how.

CHAPTER 5

Life gradually got back to normal. My ma wore black for three months; it was a tradition. People still visited all the time to express their sympathy, and pay their respects; people who hadn't been able to attend the funeral—friends and relatives from England, the States, or wherever.

My ma started looking for a job 'cos my sister Liz's income would be gone along with my da's when she got married and moved away. She'd been a housewife and mother for 26 years and it wasn't so easy, but eventually she got a part time job in a factory near us. In April, the teachers went on strike, and I celebrated my 16th birthday. My ma bought me a guitar as a way of encouraging me to have an interest in something, but our relationship had already begun to fray. I'd lost all faith in even trying to be good, 'cos the way I saw it, what good did being good do you? My da had been good, and look what happened to him.

I was getting bolder, and not obeying her rules anymore:

'Be home at ten during the week and 12 at the weekends.'

'There's nothing good on the streets after midnight.'
'Don't go here, don't go there.'

She may as well have been talking to the wall I was now sitting and staring at.

I'd started hanging around with one of my friends, *Aidan,* again. We had drifted apart after Primary school, 'cos he had gone to another school to do his Group Certificate, which took two years, and I'd gone to the Christian Brothers to do my Inter Cert, which took three. He was now working with his da. We had spent a couple of years in different gangs, but now we liked the same kinds of clothes, and the same kind of music. As he was working, he used to pay for me to go everywhere with him.

He bought Mod clothes, and got his hair cut in one of the big hair salons in town. I couldn't afford any of these things 'cos I got less pocket money since my da had died. I improvised on the clothes front though, and wore my da's mohair suits with waistcoats and braces. I changed my 'during the week' school haircut to a sort of Mod style at the weekends, with the fringe parted down the middle, and a little bit backcombed with a steel comb—the Ray Davies look. The comb also doubled as a weapon in case of emergencies. The Christian Brothers hated long hair, but being a Mod you could have short hair; all you needed was a long fringe, the steel comb for the bouffant bit in the middle, and you were transformed.

Sometimes I'd borrow clothes from *Aidan,* or one of the other like-minded boys my age, and if my ma didn't like it or wouldn't let me wear them, I'd stash them in a hedge somewhere, or down in a place we called the Valley, behind our house. I'd leave the house looking the way my ma wanted me to look on my way to a 'debate' in the school, or the 'Knights of Malta', or any other of the respectable ruses I'd use to get out of the house during the week. Then I'd change into my Mod gear, and head for the snack bar beside the Apollo cinema in nearby Walkinstown. We'd usually drink a flagon of cider from the off license, or sometimes I'd nick a couple of Librium that were left at home from some of the prescriptions my da got when he was sick.

The snack bar was great. We'd order a glass of orange or a coke and maybe some chips, depending on the financial situation, and listen to the jukebox: 'A Whiter Shade of Pale', 'Wheels on Fire', and all the hits of the time. Then we'd wait for the pictures to be over so we could check out all the chicks. We'd find out who was going out with whom, and later some of the older guys would come in after band practice—Philo, Brian, Frank and Paul—these guys were beyond Mod.

Philo, or Phil Lynott as he is better known, was singing with Skid Row at that time, and Frank and Paul were the roadies. Brian was playing drums in a different band, the Sugar Shack. They were the first real group I'd ever seen in the Moeran Hall in Walkinstown, and they were my heroes, not like the show bands my sisters used to go and see in the TV club, or the Ierne, who sang a mixture of Top 20 and country and western; all covers, no originals. These guys were the real thing. Even though they did cover the likes of The Cream, Hendrix, and the old blues greats like John Lee Hooker, Elmore James, and the rest, they also played their own originals.

Philo's group was the one I was going to see the day my da died.

They had long hair, looked really cool, and were famous in Dublin; they were eating their chips in the same snack bar as us; they were friendly; they had groupies. They were beyond Mod, they were hip. I wanted to be beyond Mod, and as hip as them.

***

I'd finally gotten to know a girl called *Nicola* then. I'd met her at the gymkhana at our school the year before, and thought she looked like the singer Julie Driscoll. She was the prettiest thing I had ever seen, in a waif-like way, and I couldn't get her out of my mind. The night after I first saw her the Beatles took part in a Europe-wide show and debuted 'All You Need is Love'. I thought they were playing it just for me. I found out to my surprise, and much to my disappointment, that she had started going out with my mate. I was heartbroken 'cos I'd fancied her forever. I thought I'd never have a chance with her.

My mate was really good looking and all the chicks fancied him. He was the first one, a couple of years earlier, to get invited down the Valley by *Tracey*. This meant more than just a casual walk to a scenic area, and everyone knew it. She was older and liked to invite some younger guys down there for a feel under her cape. He used to come back up afterwards full of stories of what he'd done, to prove he'd had a feel.

Up to that point, I'd only had a feel during games of doctors and nurses, or feeling one of the other guys' birds down the Valley. We were all curious back then, so there was a general idea that you could feel up someone else's girl if they didn't mind too much, purely for educational purposes. They'd be lying on the grass waring each other, and a couple of us who didn't have birds would be lying lower down, having a feel around. These experiences were the sum total of my sexual experience until then.

I'd never had a ware and a feel together until I met *Nicola*. I was going out with a girl called *Jen* when *Nicola* was going with my mate. I used to kiss *Jen*, French kiss her even, but it was terrible, like kissing a statue, and it never went beyond that. I used to dream about being with *Nicola*. I really fancied her and we all hung out together in a big gang. I loved being around her, and it didn't seem fair to me that she was with my mate and not me. Then, on the night of *Jen*'s 15th birthday party, my mate pulled me aside and told me *Nicola* fancied me and he fancied *Jen*, so we decided to swap girlfriends.

I was shocked and delighted that she could fancy me more than him, and going with *Jen* was just a sham. I felt really awkward with her, and uncomfortable around her and her family. She lived in one of the posh houses in Walkinstown and her father owned his own business. *Nicola* was from the corporation estate, and her father was a labourer. The contrast between them was obvious, but the real contrast came when I walked *Nicola* home and kissed her. It came so naturally. I no longer felt I was giving the kiss of life to some unconscious body, like it had felt with *Jen*. With *Nicola* it was a brand new experience. It was natural, it flowed. It was so beautiful. She looked so pale and vulnerable; she was the forbidden fruit. She looked helpless and sick, yet strong like a tomboy, in her wranglers and loafers. It was like kissing Julie Driscoll or Twiggy; she tasted like sex.

Nicola, my queen of 1968. She was animated and responsive and she gave me such a hard on, waring her against the wall at the shops before she had to go home. During the few months we were together, I got to explore more of her. I loved her and no one else was going to share her with me. Everything flowed from her. Nothing was disjointed like it had been with *Jen*, or when I'd been getting a feel without a ware down the Valley with one of the other guy's birds. Now I was getting both together. Now I could talk about stuff with the rest of the guys without lying.

I still didn't get to go all the way though; I didn't know how to get that far. I knew that I'd have to get famous first, and have groupies like Philo and the rest of them; chicks who would just look at you play and come backstage and beg you to fuck them; chicks who'd take their knickers off and say, 'Just stick it in there Shay.'

When my ma bought me the guitar, she knew I wanted to be a musician, she just didn't know why. She probably thought I wanted to be like our neighbours in the culdy, John, and Dessie, and Jimmy, who were in showbands and ballad groups. They still had daytime jobs and only played for extra money. I had no intention of combining careers. I was just going to be a star and get groupies.

I had to get my hole; I was going nuts. I didn't know how to come. I hadn't even managed a successful wank. *Nicola* used to play with it sometimes and even pull on it, but she never let me put it in her. Even when she'd play with it, nothing came out of it. I used to think it was empty. We were doing everything *but* having a ride, in laneways and in the fields.

One of the girls in her class had become pregnant, and it had been a total scandal, and she was determined it wasn't going to happen to her. Our relationship was great except for that. We'd talk about everything; our common frustrations at home, hers with her da, and mine with my ma. I was totally in love with her, but she was a virgin.

I didn't mind if that's how she wanted it to be, but I didn't want to be one too. If I could stop being a virgin, I thought, everything would be OK.

I wasn't making any progress on the music front either. I'd write songs and be able to sing them, but I could never get it together to be able to play them. John from across the culdy, who was in a ballad group, had told me the guitar my ma'd bought me was warped and wouldn't stay in tune, so I more or less gave up trying. I decided I'd stick to poetry instead. I still tried to break into the business though, and when one of the local groups, doing all the new stuff, was looking for a singer, I went for an audition. I failed because I couldn't stay in tune, and I was devastated. My dream of becoming a rock star had been dealt a severe blow. Fawning groupies seemed further away than ever.

One day, my ma came home and asked me why I wasn't playing the guitar any more. I told her it was impossible to play, that it was warped, that she'd bought me a piece of shit for my birthday. We had a big argument and I started cursing. She told me not to use such foul language, and trying to assert some kind of discipline over me, she tried to hit me. But I was too big now. I slapped her. Then I pushed her, and she fell back under the stairs. My sisters were home and they ran to help her. They were all attacking me now. I couldn't believe I'd hit my ma and pushed her under the stairs. I loved my ma. I just wanted her to let me live my own life. I had enough problems of my own without her giving me loads more. I was in shock as I stood there and watched her catch her breath. I didn't mean to hit her. It wasn't the worst thing that I'd do to her though, it was just the beginning.

***

I loved my ma just as much as my da. She was still alive and hadn't died on me or anything; she was doing her best. She was working in a factory, washing Lucozade bottles, and still doing all the housework: washing, ironing, and cooking, and here I was hitting her. She was worried about me, because she could see which way I was going long before I could.

The whole idea of my ma working in a factory was all wrong. She had always been such an elegant and ladylike person, and this had often been remarked upon to me by other people. She had just lost her husband, the only man she'd ever loved. She wanted everything for us that she'd never had, but most of all; she'd given us herself. She was a mammy, something she had never really had. Her mother had died when she was seven, and two of her older sisters had died before that from TB. My ma, who had worked since she was 14, who never borrowed a penny from anyone, who would always make ends meet whatever the circumstances, who always bought quality 'cos it paid in the long run; my ma who could have helped me through the aftermath of death, as she knew it only too well. For me it was a first death. She could have helped me and I could have helped her. But I didn't want help, I just wanted everybody to fuck off and leave me alone.

I had to push her out of my life. I wanted everyone to get out of my life and I wanted to get out of theirs. It was a couple of weeks later that I scored for the first time and nearly died. I didn't want to die but I wanted no one to die before me. I couldn't handle all that again.

***

Forget all this shit and get back to now.

I snapped out of my dreams again, back to where I was at that moment. There was all sorts of shit going on behind me. The group who had questioned me earlier like ex-junkie Gestapo officers were all running around like blue-arsed flies, shouting orders at each other like they were in the army or something.

I was being completely ignored; it was almost as if I didn't exist. Memories started running through my head again, and I could hear a little voice inside me, telling me the reality of the situation.

I feel like a right eejit sitting here looking at the fucking wall, but I've got to think things through, weigh up all the pros and cons.

Did I want to stop taking dope?

I liked getting stoned, it was really fucking nice, and I loved it. I just hated being a slave to it; a £200-a-day slave—just because I wanted a bit of peace, a peace that gets more expensive every day because there's more and more shit to forget.

There is no cure for what I've got. I don't need help. I need a fucking lobotomy.

It wasn't supposed to be like this, it was to be so simple. All you need is love; Tune in, turn on, drop out; we can change the world, and all that. I had a plan. No thoughts of the future, just the present. Paradise was going to last until I was 21, maximum, and that was going to be it. Not this sitting on a bench aged 28, waiting to beg a shower of jerks worse than myself for help.

Jaysus, how pathetic.

***

I remember the first time I scored drugs, or what I thought were drugs. I was still in school. The teachers were on strike so we had a lot of time off, and about 20 of us put our money together and scored some yellow capsules from a dealer called *Bailey* around the back of the swimming pool. It was supposed to be speed, so it would keep you bopping all night long, my mates told me. We were all in the Five Club in Harcourt Street, watching this band from Belfast called The Few, a really good blues band, but that night I had no real interest in the music.

I was just waiting to get up on the speed, and everybody else was the same. I kept asking my friend *Aidan* what was supposed to happen, as he'd tried speed before. He was trying to explain it to me.

'Your heart beats faster,' he said, 'and you feel like you're taking off to another planet, like you own the world.'

But nothing like that was happening to me. Nothing like that was happening to him either, or any of the other guys. As the night wore on, it was obvious to us we had been ripped off. We parted company, leaving for our various homes across the city, vowing to do all sorts of damage to *Bailey* before we got our money back.

The next day I was sitting in Switzer's Cafe on Grafton Street with a couple of mates from school. They'd been really impressed when a few of the music heads, who I knew from my visits to the clubs in town, had said hello to me. All of a sudden my head began to move backwards without me wanting it to. I thought it was a cramp or something and tried to bring it back up, but I couldn't. It was really weird. It was as if my head was suddenly too heavy for my neck to support. I told *Dennis*, one of the guys who was with me, what was happening and he started laughing. He thought I was joking.

He soon realised I wasn't fucking around, and I told him to grab the end of my scarf and pull my head back to the upright position. We got up and left the cafe with him walking two feet ahead of me, pulling on the UCD scarf I had on—a new version of the student look.

You should have seen the looks we were getting. He wanted to bring me to the hospital, which was just around the corner in Mercer Street, but I knew this had something to do with the shit we had taken the night before and I didn't want to be involved with anyone in authority.

He led me down Grafton Street like this and onto the bus, and sat two seats in front of me, still pulling on the scarf to keep my head from going at right angles to my body.

I was in a heap, but more worried about what might come of it all than I was about my health. I got off the bus at my stop and made it down to one of my friend's houses alone. Thank God he and not his ma opened the door, because I knew I looked really weird. His folks were really cool and were the only ones who used to let our band practice in the house, but they wouldn't have been too pleased to see me looking like this. I went into his sitting room and put my head under a drawer in the sideboard and after a while the cramp went away a bit and I was able to straighten myself out again.

My friend was freaked, too, and wanted me to go to the hospital, but I wouldn't. I went around and knocked on *Aidan*'s door but his mother told me he was in bed because he'd been sent home from work sick. She let me up to see him for a few minutes and he told me the same shit was happening to him. We both felt like we were over the worst though, and I went on home.

Later that evening, just after my ma came home from work, I began to have a relapse and it was even worse than earlier. I had absolutely no control now over my head. My sister ran over to the neighbours to call the doctor, as we had no phone, and she came back with Philip, the son who was studying to be a priest and was home on holidays. He started saying prayers over me until the doctor came.

I came clean and told the doctor what had happened, and he gave me some muscle relaxants, then went on to tell my ma I was going to die if I kept taking drugs. My ma was in a heap and I was fucking raging as I hadn't even gotten stoned.

Next day I went up to *Aidan*'s house to see how he was doing. He was really bad and, while I was there, a call came from another mate's mother to say he and one of the other lads were in the hospital and had been given the last rites; she wanted to know what we had taken. I got on the phone and explained to her how the capsules looked and the doctors were able to give them an antidote.

Luckily no one died, but altogether 15 people were treated in hospitals throughout Dublin over those few days; four in intensive care. It made headlines in the papers. For most of the gang that was the end of their experience with drugs. For me it was only the beginning: being close to death had only whetted my appetite and I felt kind of famous.

Everyone we knew was asking us what had happened; they all wanted to talk to us and hang around with us now. It was all a bit unreal, like I suddenly had this new and interesting life. I was no longer just my dead da's son, poor Shay, and I liked it.

***

Two weeks after our almost fatal experience with the bad gear from *Bailey*, we were scoring from him again. This time I made him take what he was offering first, to make sure it was OK, and this time it was real speed—Dexedrine—stolen from a local National Health Clinic. We bought 16 at a shilling each, and we dropped them that night on our way to a disco in The Core Nightclub.

Speed—proper speed—was absolutely wonderful, just like everyone said. You could dance all night and never get tired, listening to the Four Tops, The Supremes, Sam and Dave, Otis Redding, Motown … it was awesome!

By the time we got to the club we were buzzing. It was such an amazing feeling of self-confidence; all feelings of awkwardness disappeared, thoughts flowed, talk flowed, memory was aroused. I could remember every detail of everything that had ever happened to me and I wanted to tell everybody about it. All of the other guys who were stoned were feeling the same way. We were all gathered in a corner, talking ten to the dozen and all at the same time. If somebody was saying something, it was really difficult to concentrate 'cos I'd be so involved in trying to hang on to the brilliant comment I wanted to make as soon as they stopped talking. But no one wanted to stop talking. We were all talking at the same time, gathered in a corner like a load of oul ones yapping away, but it felt great.

I'd never really been shy. I'd talked in front of audiences at school debates and I used to read my poetry in the youth club on Wednesdays, but I always hated asking a bird up to dance in case they said no. My fragile ego couldn't handle the embarrassment. I'd usually just stand around wearing my dark John Lennon glasses, looking cool like nothing mattered but really hoping I'd get asked up for a ladies' choice.

That first night on speed I was transformed. I asked up a different bird for every fast set. I wasn't just hearing the music, I was feeling the music. It was in me and I could dance like I never danced before, not just the slow sets, lurching to the likes of Ray Charles' 'I Can't Stop Lovin´ You'—which amounted to getting as close as you could to a bird so she could feel your hard on for three minutes. Now I could dance to the fast songs and didn't care about the slow sets. I didn't care about getting a hard on. It was impossible anyway on speed, as my dick sort of shrivelled to nothing, but I didn't care. I felt totally awesome.

Dancing was no longer a self-conscious thing. Before I started taking speed I felt like some disjointed entity everyone was looking at for all the wrong reasons. Now it was an expression of how I felt, and how I felt was totally self-confident. I could talk to girls more easily, and keep them fascinated with all the stories I could tell. It was as if I knew everything. I didn't have any money but I had personality and I was suddenly cool, and chicks were only too glad to take me out.

It was sometimes better to hang out with the stoned guys though, because chicks never got stoned and always said they had to get home.

When we went to dances we'd have a great time, really ruling the roost, but all too soon it would be time to go and it was no fun having to go home still stoned and lie in bed until morning staring at the ceiling and listening to your little brother breathing in the bed beside yours. There were lots of things I didn't need at this stage in my life; hassles from school, and from my mother, but the one thing I definitely didn't need when I was on speed, was sleep.

We could only really afford it on weekends. Mondays were for coming down. I didn't yet know about popping a downer to combat the upper, but I'd soon learn. Sometimes, when I couldn't face going home stoned, some friends and I would walk around shooting the shit all night, until we'd all make our way to our houses and sneak in through the window and hope we didn't get caught.

***

I took advantage of the free time I had to escape from the reality I didn't want to acknowledge and the people I wanted to push away.

But the teacher's strike ended in May, and I was due to sit for my Intermediary Cert in June. Going back to school forced me to bring a bit more discipline into my life, and anyway it was only another four weeks and then the exams and the summer holidays. I had a totally different attitude to most of my mates in the class. I'd changed since the teachers' strike, and most of them seemed so boring now, and childish. In a strange kind of way they were still into football and hurling and athletics. I was beyond all that shit now. I couldn't wait for the exams to be over and the holidays to begin.

I was still going out with *Nicola* but she was only allowed out once a week and had to be home by midnight. I used to meet her after school for a couple of hours and on Friday or Saturday until midnight. She was still driving me mad with the horn when we were on our own, but she and the rest of the girls she hung around with just seemed so young now compared to the birds I'd seen in the clubs in town, and with musicians like Philo and Frank, and the older guys in the snack bar by the Apollo. I still loved her though, and I never told her about getting stoned.

The exams were over—no more school for three months—and I had a job for the summer holidays, delivering milk for Premier Dairies. It was great; I'd start at 6am and be finished by 9am, and I was getting £3 and ten shillings a week, which for me was a fortune. I'd give my ma two quid and I had 30 bob for myself. *Nicola* couldn't get a job for the summer holidays, so I'd meet her most mornings after I finished work, and we'd just hang around having a great time.

The summer of 1968 was brilliant—sunshine every day, *Nicola*, 'A Whiter Shade of Pale', money, Mods, The Kinks, The Beatles, The Who, The Small Faces and Saturday nights with my mates in Moulin Rouge, out of our heads on speed. It was perfect. I even forgot what had happened to my da.

My sister Liz got married in July. It was the last big event I remember celebrating with my family and it was a really great day.

Dave, Liz's fiancé, had a sister Aileen who was the same age as me and we were supposed to pair off at the wedding, but it never really happened. I designed my own suit and my uncle Paddy made it for me. It was in a light Donegal tweed with flared trousers and a high collared Edwardian style jacket and waistcoat, which was all the rage at the time and the kind of gear all my mates were wearing. The year before had been hipsters and crepe shirts like The Kinks, this year the Mod thing was more refined, and due to lack of funds, I had deliberately had it made so either the jacket, trousers or waistcoat could be worn with different things. That way it looked like I had loads of cool clothes.

The wedding was a blast. It was held in the Sutton House Hotel overlooking Dublin Bay on a beautiful July day. Peter gave Liz away and myself and Joey were altar boys. The mass was over by 11am and the reception started at midday. Everybody had time for a few pints before we sat down to dinner. As soon as dinner was over the band started and everybody got a chance to do their party piece. In all the songs that were being sung by my uncles, aunts and cousins, you could feel that they were a tribute to my da.

Everyone sang what they knew to be his favourite song from them; 'Spancil Hill' by my Uncle Jack, 'The Little Boy that Santa Claus Forgot' by my Uncle Christy, and so on. The highlight of the evening was just before the end when my ma sang 'It's a Sin to Tell a Lie'. It was a very poignant moment as she has a very fragile soprano voice, and it was like the words were addressed to my da:

'Be sure it's true when you say I love you,
  If you break my heart I'll die.'

It could have been a message to me, because I was on my way to doing just that; breaking my poor ma's heart. I had gone off the rails, and it was no secret that I was heavily into the drugs scene. As far as I was concerned though, I was only just beginning.

***

My first experience with eternity came pretty soon after my first brush with death from the gear we bought from *Bailey*. I couldn't blame the majority of my friends, who had the best kind of aversion therapy possible; they were now too scared out of their heads to even think about doing drugs again. But myself and *Aidan* persisted, met new friends, and got stoned at weekends, whenever there was anything available. LSD was now the catalyst. Getting stoned had become part and parcel of the whole scene that was developing.

The weekend ritual started with a trip to the launderette on Errigal Road. On Saturday mornings we'd wash our wranglers and denim jackets to get just the right fade. The afternoons were spent on marches to the American Embassy in Ballsbridge to protest against the Vietnam War, shouting, 'Ho, Ho, Ho Chi Minh, We shall fight and we shall win,' and, 'Keep America beautiful, sterilise LBJ.'

The feeling of being part of something, a movement that was growing and spreading throughout the world like a forest fire—us against them, David and Goliath—was great.

The marches were accompanied by the Gardaí, and the Special Branch was also there taking photographs of rabble-rousers and 'subversives'. It was great to be part of it and though I didn't have any really defined politics they were definitely leaning to the left.

I bought *The Thoughts of Chairman Mao* at one of these marches and could quote some of his dictums like, 'Communism grows from the mouth of a gun.'

The only gun I'd ever seen up to that point was a pellet gun, which we used to shoot at pigeons. I doubt if I ever actually hit one, and my mates were always slagging me with, 'Ye couldn't hit a barn door if you were sitting on it.'

The anti-imperialist discussions continued afterwards in the New Amsterdam cafe in South Anne Street with Pat, who was chairman of the Young Socialists, and some of the other leading young leftists. Some of them were very serious. One of the guys' reactions to smoking his first joint had been, 'Beautiful, but it's not conducive to productivity.'

Chairman Mao would have been proud of Pat. After that *Aidan* and I would meet up with *Bailey* and his mate *Paul*, who'd made a business of breaking into National Health clinics, and we'd buy the Dexedrine to keep us bopping through the night in clubs like the Five, the Moulin Rouge, or the Go-Go.

Bailey and *Paul*, his mate, had learned a lot from their first experiment as dealers, when they had nearly killed us all with the shite that made our heads go wonky. Now they wanted to keep their valued customers, as there weren't so many of them anymore. After each robbery they'd go through their medical dictionaries to make sure they were giving us the right stuff, and they personally tried all the gear themselves to make sure the dictionaries weren't lying. Sometimes they double-checked.

Knowing I was still in school and had no money—and out of a sense of guilt for nearly killing me—a lot of the time

I didn't have to pay for my Saturday night turn-on. In return I just had to introduce them to new customers; not really a difficult job as there were more and more people joining the protest marches every week, looking to get stoned like the hippies in the States who were doing the same at the end of the 1960s. I had the dealers palling up to me, customers were getting easier to find, and I'd discovered commission.

Unfortunately, that sweet little deal was not to last. Having only one regular source and a growing army of customers caused a lot of problems. The only steady supply of dope for my dealers was what they got by robbing the health clinics, and there was a limited number of them in the city. *Bailey* and *Paul* did their best to rob enough to keep the demand supplied but the Gardaí and the Eastern Health Board were making life more difficult by bolstering security. The brothers took to breaking into doctors' surgeries as well, but they never got the same quantities as when they'd done the clinics. Demand was increasing and the supply was dwindling, so *Bailey* cut out the middleman—me—and started selling direct. To make matters worse, the price went up, and more often than not I had to pay now if I wanted some for myself. Either way, I was moving on from being a casual weekend user to a regular, and I was digging myself into a hole I would find it very hard to climb back out of.

***

The strange thing is; I'd been stoned loads of times on speed before I ever smoked a joint. Back then, it was just easier for us to get, unlike now when most teenagers find it easier to get hash than to buy alcohol. Hash was irregular then, and had to be imported. There were a lot of other choices around too. I'd often been offered heavy gear like morphine, but I'd never had the nerve to try it.

I was getting seriously into the whole scene though, and was constantly on the lookout for ways to get more involved. One night *Aidan* and I were outside the Go-Go in Abbey Street. He was hoping to get a glimpse of this chick he was mad about. She was inside but we couldn't go in because we had no money, and he was hoping to catch her when she left or came out for some fresh air from the sweaty little cellar club.

We were outside the Irish Permanent Building Society office at the top of the street, where a lot of people in similar financial circumstance used to hang out, when we were introduced to a few heads from the Northside who had just come back from London. As it turned out, they had loads of 'draw' as they called it. We called it grass. They had just popped a few kilos into their woolly knitted shoulder bags and got the ferry back from Holyhead to Dun Laoghaire.

They were cool dudes. They had really long hair, down to their arses, and wore leather jackets, beautifully cut, tie-dye tee shirts, velvet pants or canvas trousers cut really tight, with flap over flies like old fashioned sailors, and stacked high-heeled snakeskin boots; gear you could only buy in one shop in Dublin, in Grafton Court—and it cost an arm and a leg. Some of that shop's best customers later became some of our best customers.

It was 1969, the year of Woodstock, and these guys looked and acted like superstars. They had chicks too—beautiful babes from Czechoslovakia who had made the escape to London after the failure of their Velvet Revolution and the invasion of Prague by Soviet tanks. These babes were just awesome. They were all older than us, 19 to 23, and they were commuters: Dublin, London, Amsterdam, Morocco. They had been around, and I was really impressed.

They laid a couple of ounces on us and said we could pay them after it was sold. 'No problem man, peace; see ye here Saturday afternoon.'

It was amazing really; I was in business again just like that. It didn't take long 'til I was wearing the same kind of clothes as them, stroked for me by my shoplifting customers in exchange for the ganja, and other harder drugs.

I got to know one of the Czech chicks quite well, but not intimately (she was the main man's squeeze and older than me in more ways than years). It was really an education talking to her about life under communism in a Warsaw Pact country, and she changed my political outlook totally. I became a right-wing hippie, so to speak, after hearing her story. I also became a full time dealer and addict.

CHAPTER 6

I had already started making promises to myself of 'never again,' that I knew I would not, and could not, keep. I'd made a promise to myself that I would never trip out on acid or anything like it again after I ended up in hospital one time. I'd bypassed the whole queue of Saturday night emergencies which were typical of a city centre hospital. I'd gone directly into casualty and they'd told me to lie on the bed and wait for a doctor. It had seemed like eternity, but this time I wanted it to end. It was a really bad trip, and now it was worse. All white sheets, and marble floors, and white suits, and everybody in white uniforms with faces like statues.

Slim, a friend who had quickly become a kind of a guru for me; longer hair, velvet pants, granddad three button vests, and no jockeys to let the babes know what length you had, was waiting outside.

We had often done this when we were tripping in the winter. If we were acid cold, cold like nothing would ever make you warm again, we'd go to casualty and pretend one of us was sick.

Aidan usually got that job as he was great at pretending he was sick. He had plenty of experience with the doctors in work; me and *Slim* had never had a real job yet. One night when we were acid cold, we had gone to Busáras bus depot early in the morning and *Slim* spent the whole time sitting on the radiator. It was burning his arse off but he was still freezing. Acid was like that—you were beyond, between, above and below the elements, and just about everything else. Now I wanted so bad to escape from eternity, as it was fucking horrible.

Slim knew I wasn't messing around this time though.

The trip had started OK. We'd done our usual Saturday night thing; sold a few painted saccharin tablets of a few different colours to our regular clientele. The pitch must have been great 'cos they came back every week.

'What would you prefer, man, the orange or the purple, the sunshine or the haze?'

As long as we had colour markers and some saccharin we were in business. We had a whole rainbow load of options. The advertising department was working like crazy during the week to think up the new names for the weekend rush. We'd always lay a little bit of draw on them so they'd think they were tripping, and it worked.

We weren't a total monopoly. We had some rivals at different corners of Grafton Street, but we had the right aura of street cred thanks to 'the bust' in Caffollas in O'Connell Street, when someone had become suspicious of a joss stick we had lit and called the drug squad. We were close to the *Irish Press* office and it made the front page.

We had taken mescalin and were tripping the light fantastic, when we were brought to the Bridewell by one of the heads of the drug squad, and one of his cohorts. It was pretty spooky being in a police holding cell. They had to let us go though, as mescalin wasn't illegal in Ireland at that time.

We took some more and went to watch *Easy Rider*, which was debuting in the Academy cinema in Pearse Street that day. I had freaked out when I thought I was queer 'cos I couldn't get it up for one of the girls who was hanging around with us at the time. My mind was elsewhere when we had gone off together, but I felt I had to try to explain it to her. The only problem was that I was trying to explain myself while we were in the Carmelite Church off Grafton Street, and all the people were queuing to get confession and saying the Stations of the Cross and the Rosary.

I'd gone in there for refuge as Grafton Street had turned into Hell. I didn't even want to be with this girl, but I still felt obliged to kiss her.

The movie itself had been really good; two guys on motorcycles with a couple of kilos of coke in the tank. The heroes had long hair, leather trousers, buckskin jackets and gorgeous gleaming chrome Harley Davidson motorcycles; the secret of success: some powder, a bike, and a couple of tabs of acid.

I don't know why I was so impressed. The only time I'd been on motorcycles before had been on a Honda 50, which belonged to a couple of the older guys on our road, and on a trip to Arklow on *Rich*'s BSA, which was ages old. It pissed down all day and I was on the back, drowned and fucking freezing.

Rich was a mate of mine. He had a job, a BSA, leather trousers, and he was totally cool.

He'd realised that *Aidan* and me were on the right path and had left the others to their showbands and Honda 50s to partake in the delights of speed and acid. But he never made it his vocation, not like me.

***

I was really freaking out now in the hospital, lying on a sterile bed, surrounded by marble and statues dressed like people in white uniforms, all whispering about me. I imagined they were just about to rape me so I jumped up off the bed and headed for the window and attempted to break it, but it wouldn't break 'cos it had little wires running through it. I knew I was in eternity then and it was horrific.

It should have been a great night; all the omens were OK, we'd sold our painted saccharin with the exotic names: Itchycoo Park, Sunny Afternoon. We were more inventive than the LSD chemist Owsley himself, or Leary, for that matter. If we'd been selling the real thing, we would have been, we could've been the *main man*—but we weren't. After we'd done our business, we had to go and see him to get the real shit.

We'd made our few quid and we went down to a pub near the inner city to score. It was one of the few pubs I could get into as they were always refusing me for being too young. I couldn't wait for my hair and beard to grow, but that was sort of impossible as I was still in school, and the head brother was really against long hair. We scored our acid and sat in the pub, drinking our pints, waiting to get up on the trip, which took a while. By the time the pub closed, we were really buzzing and we'd been having a good laugh with some of the local heads; *Tony*, *Stan*, and *Jack*, who was the brother of this girl I liked, *Alison*, and I wanted him to notice me even if she didn't. Then there was

'*The Arnold*', as one of them called himself. He was famous for tapping money for the gargle. He was sort of an upper class beggar, always looked well and drank in the best pubs, and it was always the same line; 'Can you spare a few bob for *the Arnold*?'

The other pair, *Tony* and *Stan*, were just gargle heads and weren't really into the gear. They were more into the gargle and fleadh ceoils but they had long hair and beards and used to enjoy slagging us and generally having the craic.

This pub had a few dodgy people hanging around, as well as a lot of heads into the traditional Irish music. They were really liberal when it came to the drugs. They weren't into it themselves but they didn't mind us turning on. After the pub closed, we were often invited back to *Stan*'s bedsit in Rathmines to while away the hours until dawn. I remember one night, one of the first trips I ever took, me and *Jimmy*, who was a great guitar player, were sitting, looking out the little skylight, fascinated by the night sky when I asked *Stan* for a cigarette and he said, 'Which colour would you like?' It cracked us up; it was the perfect thing to say.

Anyway, by the time we left the pub this night we were really out there. Myself and a friend called *Slim* headed down Grafton Street where we bumped into, of all people, Mick Jagger and Garech De Bruin, who owned Claddagh Records. They must have just left the Bailey or Davy Byrnes, and they were standing in the Grafton Arcade having a chat.

I was overawed and I was nearly going to ask Mick for his autograph until I started to think he wasn't real—just part of the trip. *Slim* started chatting to them, asking Mick how he liked Dublin, just small talk, and Mick was being nice and friendly.

I was speechless, as I often was when I was tripping. I used to find it hard to walk even, as it felt like I was walking on clouds or balls of mala. I think the only words I ever said when I was tripping, when asked how I was feeling, were 'It's too much man,' or 'Far out'.

We could have been standing there a minute, or an hour, or a week, or a year for that matter.

There was the usual after-the-pubs-close feeling all around. Singing and crying and rows starting or ending, when all of a sudden there was a big meleé beside us and a fray, you might say, was tumbling its way down Grafton Street.

I was in such a state of peace and love that the whole concept of fighting seemed totally alien, and I was freaking as I saw somebody break a six pack of Guinness over someone else's head. I watched the bottles break and the foam spray out in beautiful, soft, slow motion, gushing clouds as the guy's head cracked open and he started to pour blood from a volcano that had appeared in his head, and it all seemed to be happening frame by frame in slow motion 'cos that is the way things are when you are tripping. I just stood there mesmerised by the whole thing. *Slim* grabbed me and pulled me away. 'Let's get out here, man before the old bill arrives. This is a bad vibe.'

It took a while for me to sort out the confusion. I didn't want to be anywhere near a crowd after that so we decided we'd head out to the seaside. It was out near Mount Merrion when I really started to freak.

I heard some music wafting its way towards us from the blackness ahead, probably from a party or something, but I couldn't figure out where it was coming from. It just seemed to be coming from the silhouette of some trees or maybe from the trees themselves. It was probably a party going on in one of the big houses but it confused me. My head was really fucked up. I couldn't figure anything out and I just wanted to come down off this trip, there and then. I just couldn't enjoy it.

It was the same confused feeling I'd had one day out in Enniskerry, in April of the same year. The sun had been shining on one side of the road while it snowed on the other, and I was counting the millions and zillions of snowflakes as they fell, and my mates were walking ahead in the sunshine on the other side, and it was like we were in two different seasons, countries, galaxies even, but simultaneously.

We were on our way to the waterfall at Powerscourt House. We just wanted to enjoy the beautiful scenery of that part of Wicklow and pick up on the vibes, maybe become a bird, like the Indians, or some other thing inspired by one of the books we'd all begun to read, like *The Doors of Perception*. But the snow took over the other side of the road and everything went dark. We took shelter in the doorway of a little country church with a graveyard beside it.

Then *Aidan* began to freak, looking at what he thought was Colonel Mustard's gravestone. It was getting too much like the scene from *Easy Rider* when Peter Fonda's hanging from the statue of the Virgin Mary and screaming about his mother.

Now I was back in the same frame of mind, totally confused. We decided to head back to the city. To make things worse, we kept getting stopped by the Gardaí along the way. They asked us where we were going and what we were doing—the usual. It was a nightmare, and this was the state I was in when I entered the casualty; a state of eternity.

It wasn't Heaven or Hell. It was worse than Hell and it was really cold. Occupied only by statues. I could see through everybody and they were all statues, even here in the hospital. That was when I jumped up off the bed and tried to break the window, and I was thinking, *I can't stay here forever; I'm a good boy.*

Then a couple of nurses and porters grappled with me and held my arms and feet. *Slim* kept saying, 'Cool it man, you'll be alright. If you don't cool it, they'll get the old bill and you'll have to spend the night in a cell.'

I couldn't have cared less. I just wanted to be down off this trip. They pulled my trousers down and I thought, *this is it*, and then someone gave me a jab.

I don't know how long I was out, but when I woke up, my hands and feet were strapped to the bed. I was still tripping and I was strapped to the bed. I thought, *this is it man, this is it forever.* I started screaming for *Slim* and a nurse brought him in. I was begging him to open the straps and he kept saying he couldn't. I thought he was part of the whole conspiracy, that he'd arranged it all somehow, and now I was stuck here. I'd died, and this was it. My ma had come, in the meantime, with some other people, to say goodbye to it, to what I'd become.

They jabbed me with something again and the next time I woke up there was a young doctor beside my bed, reading me a book: *The Teachings of Don Juan.* I was still strapped but calmer, and it was daytime and the sun was shining. The doctor was one of the guys who had attended a lecture about the effects of LSD a few of us had been asked to take part in at the College of Surgeons, several months before.

We'd been approached by someone doing research, who obviously knew where to look for people who used it.

At the time none of us had a bad word to say about it. In fact, some of the students were so impressed they wanted to buy some afterward. One of them accompanied us through many interesting drug experiments later, and became our link to a higher class of client. He too became a junkie, and a consultant on all types of synthetic opiates.

When he finished reading, he asked me if I was OK. I think he could see his reading and the medicine had had the desired effect, and he opened the belts and they let me go.

I walked down to Stephen's Green with *Slim*, and he was saying, 'Man, you really had me worried then.'

But I wasn't really listening. I felt changed; I never wanted a trip like that again. I was going to be a good boy from now on.

It was only a short walk from the casualty in Vincent's Hospital to St Stephen's Green, but I had been released from an eternity worse than Hell, worse than the Devil or even Jesus in his final moment of unforgiving humanity. I was going to be a good boy and be good in school and admit I was wrong. I wanted to be surrounded by the monotony of Maths and Physics and questions 'cos the answer to everything was beyond description. It was just me and me.

I stayed in my bed most of the time after that, for three or four months. My ma was glad I was home. I just didn't talk and wore black clothes, in an effort to say something, I suppose. I didn't want anyone to know what happened in the never-ending future.

After a few months I got better, and one Saturday night, *Aidan* called for me and I went out with him. As usual, he had the money and it was to be a night on the town. He had been through his shit and I'd been through mine and now we were just going to be teenagers; 17 years old and not a care in the world.

When I got into town and started hanging out outside one of the pubs near Dame Street, I felt like I'd betrayed the movement. I had short hair now. I met two girls I used to know well, and they didn't recognise me. When they asked, 'How are ye doing man?' I knew they knew the answer 'cos they'd been to see *Easy Rider* the same day as me. They knew I wasn't stoned but really fucked up now, and I was glad when *Eddie* came by and laid a few Tuinal on me.

Some people said he was crazy; one of the *Mad Eddies* — three mates, all called *Eddie* and capable of almost anything. I remember when someone set an Alsatian on them in St Stephen's Green, and they'd all ended up diving on the bowler instead, and biting it until it ran away, scared out of its life. I was glad of the Tuinal. It wasn't a drug; it was the pillow over my head. I didn't want to get stoned. I just wanted to be out of my head. I took them all and was almost instantly brain dead.

It was beautiful; an instant cure for eternity.

Somehow or other, something or someone wanted to wake me from the fuzzy, tingling escape in which I was enveloped, in a place beyond. I woke up in the hallway of the Fleet pub in Fleet Street before closing time. I had to communicate with someone I trusted, so I called that girl *Alison* who I'd been obsessed with all this time. Even though she didn't want to know, I knew some part of her would want me to stay alive, so I called her with my last grasp of the real world. She sent *John*, her older brother, down from the pub to collect me, and he brought me to *Stan*'s place. He looked like Jesus with a bit more anger, and he'd saved me from beyond eternity.

When I woke up, there were footprints all over my jacket. I'd fallen asleep in a doorway somewhere, before someone had dragged me into the pub hallway for my own safety. It was a lesson I'd always forget.

***

Back on the bench in Coolmine again, I tried to think clearly. *What were my options?* I could get up and leave, get a bus into town, meet *Jodie*, and be stoned within an hour. She'd be glad I'd left there just to be with her. We could make arrangements to get out of Dublin; anywhere but London, as I still had a warrant out for my arrest there.

We could go to Europe, maybe somewhere warm. But then there was the other option; I could stick this out, get clean, start living a proper life. To do that, I would have to struggle through this addiction.

Cold Turkey. I'd done it before; stayed off for four and a half years, I could do it again. I don't need therapy, I just need to get away from Dublin, from the whole mad scene; the drugs families, Rathmines, Ranelagh, Fatima Mansions, just out of the trap, out of the hole I'd dug for myself.

I was still looking at the sign: No drugs, no chemicals, no alcohol of any kind, no violence or threats of violence—thinking of my options.

The court cases were coming up soon, with several charges of fraud and possession with intent to supply heroin, not much heroin, just enough to keep me going for a couple of days. The copper who had busted me knew I wouldn't sell it for all the rice in China, but he wanted to do me because of my relationship to the hoods, the real movers and shakers, and he knew he could send me away for a long time.

One of my mates had just gotten 14 years for a couple of kilos of hash. Even if I did a runner they'd put an international warrant out for my arrest, so I could never go back to Ireland again. I was thinking of anybody who could help me; my mother, brothers and sisters, my old girlfriend, still thinking: *What the fuck am I going to do?*

As I sat on the bench I thought about a lot of things. It was sort of like dying I suppose, watching your life flash by just before you expire. I thought about some of the people I knew who had been through Coolmine—not just people I vaguely knew, but people I had really known, like *Willo*, who had finished a course out there and who *did* remain clean for a while.

It was probably the only time he was straight since he'd been a teenager, but after a while he went back on the needle. It was just weekends at first but it didn't take long until he was back to square one.

He had spent 14 months in there and managed to stay straight for six months. Shit, I had done better than that without any treatment, just cold turkey and then four and a half years clean.

***

Why was it that so many people who got involved in dealing ended up sampling their own wares? Before they knew it, they were hooked. That's how I got into it. By 1968 I had tried a lot of drugs, and was passing on more to anyone I knew, but then this guy who knew one of my mates came over from England with a lot of morphine. As he didn't know anybody higher up in the food chain, it fell to me to move his 'product' for him, through some of the people I had met at marches and around town.

I liked the idea of being the guy to go to, the main man, so I took on the task happily. It was great being seen as someone so cool he was ahead of everybody else, because what we were peddling with morphine was a lifestyle that didn't yet exist in Ireland.

Of course I had to try the stuff several times before I was sure it was suitable for the people I was going to sell it to, and that was where it all started to go downhill. After you take an opiate like morphine, there is rarely a chance to turn back. It grabs you and sucks you under like a wave, and most people never get to come up for air.

That first time I took it, I was sick all over the place. I had been trying hard to play it cool, to act casual as if this was something I did every day. Soon it would be, but at that stage I was a complete novice to drugs like this.

I'd clumsily filled the syringe and easily found a vein I couldn't miss—my arms were still pristine—but I was as nervous as anything, not so much because of what was about to happen, but because I didn't want to slip up. In a way, I was looking forward to the trip.

When I slid the needle into my arm I winced at the initial pinch of pain, but I was mesmerised by the sight of the morphine emptying into me, tinged with my blood as I pressed down on the plunger.

The initial hit knocked me for six. I felt a sharp, tingling, burning sensation in every fibre and cell of my body, before I was swept away in a rush of absolute euphoria. No other drug I had taken could equal the sensation; it was pure joy, and I felt it all over. That was quickly followed by a strange sense of feeling totally cocooned, completely safe, as if I was wrapped inside my own little world where nobody, and nothing, could intrude.

As with all opiates, the natural reaction of my body was to reject the drug coursing through my veins, and I threw up a couple of times, but almost straight away any feelings of illness were swept away by a return to that blissful state of ecstasy.

I lay on the floor of someone's flat for hours, but it seemed like days, and I never wanted to leave the blissful state I was in.

After I took it, I knew I had found the drug I had been looking for. It let me escape from my life, to shelter myself away from everybody whenever I wanted. I took it a few more times in the next few weeks, and I liked it more and more each time. I could see which way I was heading, but I didn't care. How could anything that good be bad?

I was also gathering a lot of street cred, which unfortunately was something I was looking for in my life. It was a big ego boost, not only to be the guy who had shot-up morphine, but to be the guy who could get you some if you wanted to try it too.

It would be a while before I moved onto heroin, but only because it wasn't available to the likes of me just yet. Soon it would be, but it wasn't until I was in London a few months later that I was able to get myself seriously into a habit. Once you become addicted, it is very hard to get out of it, as many of my friends would find out.

***

Yeah, two of the guys I knew who had finished the treatment had fucked up in a short space of time, one of them bringing me down with him. I kept on staring at the wall, thinking. And then there was *Bill*; he had been through Coolmine twice.

We had run off to London together when we were 17, as Dublin had gotten a little too small for us. We wanted to hit the big smoke and we knew we could get a steadier supply of all manner of drugs over there, without the hassle we had in Dublin.

We set out for London to see the Rolling Stones' free concert in Hyde Park. We had about £5 each after we got off the ferry in Liverpool so we'd made our way to Blackpool, as it was summer and it was the nearest seaside resort we knew about. We'd both been using a lot of drugs, but we were still into bands and chicks and looking good. Things had been bad in Dublin for both of us, not just because of the law, but because of the whole scene. We had attended the funeral of one of our mates, *Col*, just before we left. It was to be the first of many funerals!

Col was a great guy. He had short, jet black hair and a bushy beard. He was one of the gang from Ballyfermot. There were gangs from all parts of the city and all with the same ideas.

Col was the first one to die. He had great credentials, as his da worked as a cook in a police station. Every time he'd been busted he'd been put under pressure not to jeopardise his da's job, and consequently the rest of his family, but he had never grassed anyone up.

There were about ten of us living in the same pad on Rathmines Road when he died. We had all told him to go to the doctor or go into hospital because we could see he was sick. Hepatitis was becoming a common threat for all addicts. Loads of people had it at the same time, but *Col* looked really sick, because the yellow of his skin and eyes contrasted so much with his dark hair and beard. We had all been sharing the same works and spikes, but there was no great panic that we'd all kick the bucket. A couple of us had had a touch of jaundice, but none of us got Hep like *Col*, and I didn't get sick at all.

His funeral was a weird affair, with two sets of mourners: his parents, brothers, sisters, aunts, uncles and neighbours, all very sad and grieving as he was only 18; and us, a motley crew from all over the city, there to pay respects to our first martyr, our very own James Dean.

We had just wanted a bit of peace, away from the rat race and the manic hustle and bustle of life and work and family and everything that comes with them, and *Col* had found his. He had wanted to escape from Christian Ireland, and all the bad memories it had forged in his brain. He wanted to finally get away from the Christian Brothers who'd been entrusted with our education, the very ones who'd battered us across the ears when we made a mistake in our irregular French verbs, teaching us languages while making us deaf. He'd escaped from the nuns who taught us music, smacking a ruler across our fingers when we made a mistake. Sadists rearing masochists, is how he saw it—that was Christian Ireland.

Col had always been talking about cycles: 'Turn, turn, turn, there is a season ...' and now his was complete.

He knew he was dying and he didn't give a fuck. He was ending a cycle and he was the first with the way out. None of us gave a fuck about anything and at *Col*'s funeral we weren't sad or anything, except maybe for his girlfriend, because she had his kid. I was a little bit upset in Deansgrange cemetery, though, when *Bailey* and *Paul* jumped into the open grave beside his and danced in it, after his family had gone. It made me think about my da's funeral a year before. But I knew *Bailey* had the dope for the party afterwards. I didn't get too upset.

It was a great wake, celebrated mainly in the toilet of a pub on the corner of two streets in Dublin city centre. We chose it because it was the one we were least likely to be barred from.

The jacks were down the stairs and it was difficult for the barman to see how often you were taking a leak. It was also easy to sneak in someone who was already barred, for a quick turn-on. The gear wasn't great, mainly Tuinal and Nembutal—sleeping pills—but they were effective, like drinking 25 pints in one gulp, and it hit the same part of your brain in the same microsecond. After taking them, you would no longer notice, or care, that you were falling down the stairs instead of walking, or letting whoever happened to have the works try to get you a hit, in their own state missing more often than not, and for the next few days you could proudly display your abscessed arms like badges of courage. The next day you could pay a visit to the drug unit in Jervis Street Hospital to have bandages applied, and then return during the week to have them removed, in the hope that you might meet someone with something to sell before the weekend, something that might turn you into a junkie.

It was hard to show your disillusionment with society if you weren't stoned. Not everyone could appreciate the beauty of the bluish-green circles emanating from somewhere near a missed vein, showing your power over life and death. Most people didn't understand: stupid cunts. They were afraid to die.

Myself and *Bill* were too, to an extent. I supposed it was the same with everybody, but at least we talked about it. He wasn't sure he wanted to spend the rest of his life dying, even if he was getting stoned. He liked me enough to introduce me to his ma, da, sisters and brother. I talked to them like I talked to my neighbours when I was doing the church collection, even though I was ripping them off. I was normal and had a family similar to his: an older brother and two older sisters.

His older brother and mine had a lot in common, his was into politics, mine was into religion. His sisters were the same as mine; eye candy to all the neighbours, one of them in particular, who was older than me but inspired many a wank. He had a ma and da and he hated his da as much for living as I did mine for dying.

He had no younger brothers and sisters as I had, so there was no reason for him to be setting a good example. His ma and da preferred me to all of his mates, ones that he'd known most of his life. They'd only known me a few months but apparently I could yap away about anything and 'seemed like a nice lad'.

***

Not grassing people up was obviously an important thing for us. It was like an unspoken rule that if one of us got caught by gardaí, we took the rap and didn't grass on anyone else. If you did, it might be the last thing you did, because sooner or later, the main men running the whole drugs show in Dublin would hear about it, and that would be the end of you.

I'd moved out of my ma's at this stage because it was getting too difficult to make any real money or stay stoned as long as I wanted when I was still living at home. It wasn't long after that when I got busted for the first time. I was charged with possession and intent to supply morphine.

As I was still only 17, and had no previous convictions, I got probation, but the let-off didn't make me take any heed of where my life was going. It was with this in mind that *Bill* and I had headed to England together. The Rolling Stones playing in London was only the start of our plan, or lack of it. We just wanted to get there and see what happened. When his parents found out he was gone, it was surely some comfort for them to know he was with 'that nice lad Shay' at least.

***

After the few quid ran out in Blackpool, the chicks didn't really appreciate who we were and we had to start buying them drinks. We weren't familiar with the town and didn't know where to go where people would notice that *Bill* looked like cutting edge musician Edgar Broughton and I looked like somebody vaguely famous. All the birds were looking for Elvis or Billy Furey lookalikes. *Bill* didn't have much choice about who he looked like, as he had tight curly hair beginning to grow into an Afro, and it didn't make any difference anyway, as we both ended up under a pier, broke.

We were woken up by a couple of coppers some time in the early morning; they weren't looking for us, just doing their rounds. They searched us and found nothing—no contraband and no money—which was the bad part. It's an offence to have nothing, as in no visible means of support, although we didn't know it then.

The only thing they'd found that interested them was a cutting from the *Evening Press* in Ireland, about *Col* being busted for indecent exposure at a Fleadh Ceoil (he'd been taking a piss after drinking a few flagons of cider, long before he'd gotten into the gear). By the time the case came to court he was well into drugs and the journalist, making the most of this fact, had written, 'Junkie gets six months for indecent exposure.'

He was out on bail awaiting appeal when he died. I don't know why *Bill* had the newspaper cutting in his pocket, but it was enough reason for the coppers to take us in.

Luckily they only kept us for a couple of hours. They checked us out and as we weren't wanted anywhere they let us go. They didn't bust us for 'no visible means', which was a stroke of luck; they just told us to get out of Blackpool and dropped us off at the city outskirts, like in the cowboy films. We could continue our journey to see the Stones.

***

Jesus, me and Bill went back a long way. It was 1981 now, and we had done a lot of shit together, even after his first time in Coolmine. He had fucked up after about three weeks, and went on a rampage but had gone back in there and was now the top member of the staff.

We used to see each other when I was straight but I hadn't spoken to him since I got strung out again. I'd tried but he refused to take my calls. It was like I had contracted leprosy or something. In a way, I suppose I had; heroin addiction was social leprosy.

CHAPTER 7

Londonondon was like 20 cities in one, with loads of Grafton Streets. Dublin was nothing in comparison. Here, everybody looked cool, at least everybody where we went: Piccadilly, Leicester Square, Kensington Market, Derry and Tom's Roof Garden Restaurant in Kensington High Street, The Greyhound in Fulham Palace Road and the Roundhouse in Chalk Farm.

There were cool heads everywhere and everybody wanted to get stoned—tune in, turn on, drop out. It was so simple when you had the vibe. You just had to feel it man. It was everywhere but most people couldn't see it. They were blind. Everyone over 20 was blind. I was never gonna go blind unless I could be blind like Willie McTell, with the blues roaring out of my smoke filled lungs and scorched throat, searing through the souls of millions. If I couldn't do it like Willie, I was gonna be dead before I'd be blind at 20.

There were certain pieces of reality still to be dealt with though, certain necessities, and number one was looking cool. *Bill*, my mate *Aidan*, and I, had to look cool enough for the customers we picked outside the pub on Piccadilly

Circus. Number two was that we had to earn a living, and get enough money together to keep ourselves in gear, so we kept ourselves busy with a good scam. Piccadilly was the ideal place for our business, with a front door on the Circus, and crucially, a back door leading on to Shaftesbury Avenue.

Anyone with hair approaching their shoulders and looking like a tourist was qualified, as far as we were concerned. While the rest of the hippies were lying in the sun under the statue of Eros, we were getting busy.

'Wanna score any dope, man?'

'Give me the bread. I'll be back in five minutes with the gear. My mate'll stay with you until I'm back.'

Aidan and I took turns staying with the customer.

'Look normal, man. Take a photograph or something,' we'd say, creating a bit of paranoia in the customer so as to precipitate a quick handover of the cash. Then we'd make a slow walk down the stairs of the pub and a quick run up the back stairs; and a trot to the chemist on Shaftesbury Avenue.

'Two packets of asthma tobacco, please.'

We'd quickly break out the asthma tobacco on the way back and wrap it in tinfoil, rush down the Shaftesbury Avenue stairs of the pub, and walk coolly up the Piccadilly Circus exit.

'Here you go, man. Peace. Watch out for the pigs.'

It was better than Grafton Street, a kind of permanent Saturday night. There were always new customers, although we did get the odd few—who obviously liked getting stoned on the asthma tobacco—who came back for more.

We were new on the Dilly Circus but it didn't seem to bother anyone who was more established than us. There were enough customers for everybody. It was the perfect scam really, as we were making the kind of money real dealers made, but we had none of the risks. We never had any contraband and we didn't have to smuggle. In fact, we weren't breaking any laws at all. We didn't have to worry about the Old Bill. The only people we had to worry about were the customers we'd ripped off. And the chances of us seeing most of them again were very slim. We mostly sold to tourists and there were plenty of those around Piccadilly Circus.

We did of course get the odd discerning customer who wasn't into grass and wanted to score some nice Moroccan or Paki Black. These guys seemed a bit cleverer than the usual tourists so we'd turn them over to another couple of Irish guys who'd been into this scene for years in London. They did a nice little business in bum hash which they cooked themselves. It really looked and felt like the real thing, as long as it was fresh. Once it was a couple of days old it got stale and hard, and was useless. After we got to know the lads better, they let us in on the recipe.

It was quite simple really: ground bay leaves, Bisto, the whites of eggs and black pastel crayons. The quantities depended on how many kilos we wanted to produce. There was a bit of preparation, too. In order to get the right flaky effect when baked, the ground bay leaves needed to be sifted through tights, in order to remove all the husks. Most evenings after finishing our shift and scoring a couple of packs in Gerard Street, we'd head back to whatever squat we were occupying, and start cooking. *Aidan* turned out to be quite a master chef in this regard. He was able to judge correctly the right amount of egg white for the right amount of bay leaves and Bisto. The black pastel crayon was for painting the outside black, right after it came out of the oven. The crayon more or less melted over the greeny, yellowy cake. Then we were in business again for the next day with our Paki Black, Lebanese Gold and Zero Zero Moroccan. We had even begun to burn our own brands into the cakes, to add a bit of authenticity.

We were making a nice living doing this, but the coppers weren't idiots and didn't just turn a blind eye. They were waiting for a change in the fraud law which would allow them to bust people for fraudulently misrepresenting hashish or grass. Unfortunately for us, the law was passed. It was a bizarre state of affairs but we could now be busted for possessing or selling legal substances, because we were fraudulently presenting them as illegal substances. It was now possible for us to be done for baking or possessing our bay leaf cakes. As most of the coppers from Vine Street Station knew us to see, we decided to get out of the business for a while.

After I had gotten into morphine back in Dublin, I'd found myself surrounded by people who had heroin to offer, and because I had loved the feeling and sensation of pure joy and comfort, I wanted to give it a shot. It was different, but to me it was just as good. There were no burning, tingling sensations, but I felt cocooned from reality, and still felt the waves of joy flood through me whenever I stuck a needle into a vein. Pretty soon I went from a casual user to a habitual one, and the waves of pleasure grew shorter, as did the time between each fix.

We had been scoring heroin every day in Gerard Street for over a year now. Out habits had gone from casual to hardcore and we were shooting up at least once a day. We were officially junkies. Because we were there so often, we had become trusted by most of the people involved in selling smack. As soon as they heard we were out of the rip-off hash business, we were offered jobs as runners for one of the big heroin dealers. It was a Canadian chick and her room mate who had offered us the gig. We were among their best customers, and she knew from the amount of money we were spending with her every day, that we could hustle. She could trust us, too, as we'd been scoring from her all the time, and she hadn't had any problems with the Old Bill up to that point. She wanted to get away from hustling on Gerard Street herself.

Our job was to be pretty easy. Each day we would call and find out which tube station they would be in and what platform and what times they'd be there at. We then made our way down Gerard Street and steered the customers in the right direction. For every five packs sold, we got one. There were other dealers on Gerard Street but this Canadian chick had the best reputation, as the gear she sold was the least cut and the best value for the ill-gotten gains of the customers. They didn't mind travelling a little bit, as long as they were sure of the best turn-on, and working this way with the underground system seemed the best way to guarantee a steady supply. The chances of getting busted were really slim.

However, all good things come to an end, and so it was with this chick and her friend. Her supplier, *Billy*, was on bail awaiting an appeal to the High Court. He'd been sentenced to seven years on a possession with intent charge, and had appealed it. The chances were that he would get a few added on. He had been the first to be busted in London with Chinese heroin 18 months earlier. Up to then, there was a plentiful supply of over-prescribed pure pharmaceutical smack on the market. Due to media campaigns against maverick doctors, writing prescriptions for heroin for anyone who came into their surgery and asked for one, regardless of whether they were strung out or not, the law had been changed. The plentiful supply of English H had dried up, and some young Asians like *Billy* had taken up the slack.

It was a guy from Dublin, named *Tommy*, who had been the first to score from one of these guys. Up to then, it had been only used by the Asians in their homes and clubs on Gerard Street. Since that time, it had become an epidemic, and the Canadian's supplier had become the first major dealer. He had just decided to accumulate enough money before he started doing his time.

When he lost his appeal it was the beginning of the end for us. The girls picked up another Asian supplier but the bags got smaller as their habits got bigger. The customers noticed the drop in quality and weren't prepared to go through the whole rigmarole on the tubes, in order to end up scoring the same shit they could score from anyone else on the street. The number and quality of the bags we were getting as commission was getting less and less, and became nothing after the girls decided to go back to selling it themselves on Gerard Street.

You could always tell a dealer was taking too much of their own shit if you saw them on the streets trying to sell it.

Aidan and I had led a charmed life up to that point. We'd managed to get stoned every day for months on end, just by giving people directions—just like any decent copper would, when asked. However, we had major habits now. We were well and truly addicted. It had just sort of happened—one day we were tripping and having a great time floating around London without a care in the world, and the next we were strung out and desperate for a fix half the time. Our habits had gone from casual to serious, and costly, and now we needed to hustle for our dope like all the rest of the junkies.

We started baking hash again and hustling down at the Circus, but it was winter now and it was really difficult to find, never mind hustle tourists, especially when you were sick with stomach cramps and pains in every fibre of your body. People tended to avoid you too, if you looked like death warmed up. Our sunken eyes and gaunt faces betrayed us before we could even open our pitch to anyone approaching. We were ill, and we both knew it.

That was all we ever did now—talk about how sick we were. We were 19 and all we ever talked about was being sick. There was only one medicine for the sickness and when we weren't shooting it, we were talking about it or how we'd get money to get more of it. The only certainty was that we would get more of it, any way we could.

It was a 24-hour-a-day job. As soon as you spent the money to get stoned, you went looking for the money for the next turn-on. It was easier to rob, rape and pillage when wrapped in the warm blanket that kept every cell in your body safe, no matter how many times a day they were at risk.

We had a nice safe respectable squat in Kentish Town, a 'Green Nigger' part of London. This was very important, not just as a secure base, but also because you could buy Major cigarettes, an essential part of enjoying *the goof*. Most of our peers, who hadn't become strung out, couldn't understand how that was so enjoyable but the goof was what it was all about. When you could get enough dope in you to be suspended between awake and asleep; where sleep could break into awake at any given moment, in the middle of the most important statement you were ever going to make in your life; or when you were having a smoke after a really good fuck; or cooking the dinner or tomorrow's ganji.

Awake could attack sleep in the same way; like when the newspaper you were reading went on fire, or your smoke burned your finger and you knew you needed more pain killer and cooked some more up on a spoon—the beautiful brown shit. You'd do anything to keep it coming, and to avoid having to wait for it.

I got so bad that at one stage I used to walk around all day with a big long needle stuck in my groin so that I could just pop a works full of 'brown sugar' in without having to spend hours looking for a vein and coaxing it to life. The syringe was just like part of my body. For lack of a really long needle that was sure to hit that vein and might hit an artery, maybe you could risk one in your dick—not all the time, but sometimes, or maybe even all the time, as it was better than a good fuck, and you were going to be dead soon anyway. That's why it was important to have a safe base to do all this stuff in. It was risky to do most of it anywhere else. I mean, you couldn't walk around Piccadilly Circus with a needle stuck in your penis.

We knew that, 'cos a lot of people we knew had been busted in all kinds of public places. I had almost become a victim myself, during the second time when we were selling the bum hash. I hadn't been prudent enough to keep a little bit for the morning, and I'd been working straight for a few hours before I'd scammed this French guy for £40 worth of Nepalese temple balls. The gear was still fresh and temple balls were still a possibility after a particularly loquacious pitch. As soon as I had the poke, I legged it up to Gerard Street and scored a £20 bag. I was so eager for a turn-on that I went into the public jacks on the junction of Shaftesbury Avenue and Tottenham Court Road.

I'd barely managed to close the door, when some copper kicked it open and dragged me out. I hadn't even had time to open the bag. I'd just dropped it with the shock, and I could see it on the white tiles. It looked as big as a packet of smokes to me, so conspicuous, just screaming out to be seen and picked up by the copper with an 'Ello, 'ello, 'ello.'

I was willing it to disappear as the copper searched and searched but I was blessed; the cunt was blind.

He and his partner brought me down to Vine Street to check me out on the computer. All I had on me was a works, a brand new one with no traces, and after a couple of hours, they let me go. I was cheeky and desperate enough to go back to the same toilet afterwards, and I found the pack. I popped it into a condom, stuck it in my mouth, and found a real safe place to jack it up. It felt extra good.

***

When we first arrived in London we had lived in squats in Earl's Court and in Haverstock Hill in Hampstead. They had been back in our pre 'totally strung out' days, when smack was just one of the many pharmaceuticals we ingested. We still wanted to have a life back then, check out a new film in the West End, like *Clockwork Orange* or *Last Tango in Paris*; or go to a gig in the Marquee in Wardour Street, or the Greyhound in Fulham Palace Road, or the

Roundhouse in Chalk Farm, or an all-nighter on Fridays or Saturdays in the Lyceum.

We were still free then, and could make decisions based on whims. When we had made a particularly nice deal, like a half a kilo of our homemade hash, we might even head up to Kensington Market and buy a new pair of platform snakeskin boots, a new pair of velvet strides, or a crepe shirt. Then we'd head down for a cup of coffee in the rooftop restaurant in Derry and Tom's, and maybe later get stoned. If it happened to be good quality smack that we chose, the likelihood was that we'd still be throwing up in the bog after every turn-on, as our young bodies were still trying to reject the shit.

We could even afford to be broke sometimes, and just go and lie in Regent's Park on a hot sunny day, exposing our skinny white torsos to the sun, playing with Frisbees, feeling our long hair licking our shoulders and checking out all the babes; and maybe even score with some chick named Penny or Sue or Priscilla. We were free then. Getting stoned was just part of the whole lifestyle. It wasn't everything. There was always something happening and loads of things to do—even without poke. There were free art exhibitions, free concerts, and free band practice. We'd regularly go and see the Jeff Beck Band practising in the Country Club in Hampstead, just around the corner from our squat on Haverstock Hill.

That had been a particularly unsafe squat. It was unsafe because you never knew what was gonna happen next. We were one of the first residents when it still had an operational telephone, for example.

There had only been five of us originally. Firstly *TJ*, who had opened it up, as that was his thing. He was a little bit older than us and looked like a Red Indian with jet black hair down past his arse, and parted in the middle. He was about six feet two and looked regal. He was authoritative. He had a London accent, as he had lived there since he was four, but he'd been born near where I was from.

Then there was his girlfriend, or should I say a chick who thought she was his girlfriend, named *Ash*. She was 15 and from some town outside London, in Kent. She looked much older, was tall with nice legs, accentuated by hot pants, and had big tits. She also looked like she was in the wrong place, a different era, or a scene from a different play. There was me and *Aidan*, and *Craig* from Glasgow, who looked like he was from Glasgow. He had a job. We all had a room each, a mattress, and a sleeping bag. There was a cooker and a fridge and a TV, all of which had been provided by the Squatter's Association, who believed in free accommodation for everybody, and even hooked up the electricity and the water, all for free. These people were some radical hippies who made shit happen, and were loosely affiliated with similar groups in other cities like Berlin and Amsterdam.

TJ was an essential member of this movement. He was great at spotting houses and buildings which could be taken over and given to the people, and he was respected all over London. He had been instrumental in opening up one of the most famous of all squats near Piccadilly, where hundreds of people were living. He was famous everywhere, as the residents had violently resisted all attempts to move them and it made the headlines all over the world.

This particular squat in Haverstock Hill became famous because of its close proximity to a gig venue. It was only 200 yards away, if that. Some entrepreneur had managed to get hold of a big Victorian building and turn it into a concert hall. It was open once a week, on Sundays, from 2pm until midnight. There was always a good line up—two upcoming bands and a headliner. Bands like the Pretty Things, Hawkwind, The Edgar Broughton Band, and Thin Lizzy. In between bands, an American DJ named Jeff Dexter used to play some of the best sounds around. It was also a Mecca for the out-of-townies, who had come to the Big Smoke to score some dope, to take them through the week out in the sticks.

At the venue we used to sell real drugs, as we were there every week and our customers knew it. It was mostly an acid, sulphate and qualude type of clientele. It was for most people a time of experimentation, of tripping out and opening themselves to new experiences. Everybody wanted to be turned on and tuned in to the vibe of the time.

The promoters catered for everything, including a mini hospital with hippie doctors for people having bad trips, or heavy paranoia attacks, or even fainting. A very popular drug with the patrons, though not the management, was Mandrax or Randy Mandies as they were more popularly known, as it made it easier to get into a chick's knickers if she'd popped a couple of them. Personally, I preferred them when they at least appeared to be alive.

The reason the promoters frowned on Mandies was that they gave the place a bad name. Anyone found dealing them inside was instantly barred, so all the dealing was done outside. The great advantage of Mandies was that they only cost a pound for two, so anybody could afford them, even the kids who couldn't afford to go in. Dropping a couple of Mandies was like drinking a couple of bottles of vodka in the space of a minute. They were from the Qualude family of hypnotic sleeping pills and turned you instantaneously into a wobbling heap of jelly, unable to stand, walk, talk, drink, eat, think or anything else necessary to survival.

The only thing possible after these things was standing, wobbling and falling down, and this is what the average Londoner, walking or driving by the venue on a Sunday afternoon, saw: lots of young kids, standing, wobbling and falling, some of them standing, wobbling and falling down the 40 or 50 steps which led to the entrance. It was like some kind of avant garde street ballet.

I never got into Mandies. The place on Sundays was a pure speed day for me. It was imperative to be awake for the highlight of the week. It was really good when Thin Lizzy played, as it was like a reunion—all the heads from Dublin, like some elite club.

Every week, after the venue, we would have a new arrival in our house. Anyone who got invited, for whatever reason, would just stay. It was that kind of place. It was that kind of feel; a real community vibe, where we were all supposed to be in together. Whatever had been going on in your life before you arrived was just forgotten. This could get out of hand at times though. The bedrooms; every inch of them was full of bodies. *Craig* from Glasgow, one of the original gang of five, now had a girlfriend, and he moved into the kitchen for a bit of peace. *Aidan's* girlfriend arrived from Ireland and *Bill* moved in after spending a few weeks with his sister, who was married now and living in Wimbledon. It was total chaos. One of the new arrivals was a guy called *PJ*. He had all the right credentials—tall, long hair, an essential badge of courage and an attest to the amount of time one had been in this frame of mind. He got involved in all the shit that was going on, like he'd been weaned on it.

The house had become pretty wild now, and sometimes I had to leave it just to look at the real world. It had gotten out of control. I hadn't dropped acid for a long time, but sometimes weird shit happened that made me feel like I was tripping. One Sunday, *PJ* didn't come back from the gig venue. Not unusual; people left sometimes for days, but not *PJ*. He arrived back two days later. No one knew how.

It was like he'd dropped from somewhere 'cos he didn't look like he was in any position to make his own way home. His hair had been chopped off, like with a garden shears. It was left in tufts on his head, like an urchin with alopecia. He just stood in the corner, with one hand permanently scratching his head and his hand covering his face as if from a blow. His other hand was covering his balls, and one foot was standing on the other, while one knee was crooked over the other. It was *PJ* though. It was his face, and his piercing brown eyes, but there was nothing going on behind them. *PJ* had left. His body couldn't talk, or walk, or sing like it used to. It couldn't laugh or play or roll a joint or get stoned. His mechanism had gone. That was *PJ*'s last trip.

We didn't know much about him, just his Christian name. He'd only been with us a few weeks, and he wasn't very free with information about himself. Consequently, nobody asked, as personal details usually came out if any sort of trust was built; but he'd just arrived and had kept very much to himself. We did know he was from some suburb in London, and on searching his bag, we found the phone numbers of some people and made some calls. We felt it was better not to call the cops, as he looked so frightened, and we didn't want to make it any worse. The medical profession was also not held in very high esteem by us, except perhaps for the head doctors, who were at the gig venue every week. *TJ* took it upon himself to find out who *PJ*'s contacts were. We all agreed that he should be handed back to his family, if he had one, and we all took turns at talking to him, and reading, and playing nice music, trying to elicit some kind of reaction; trying to find the *PJ* who had left on Sunday. After three days, we finally located his older sister, and she came and collected him and brought him home.

It wasn't the same anymore after that. I knew I'd been close to where *PJ* went—a couple of times. There were so many people living there now and all sorts of niggly arguments were going on: who stole who's food from the fridge, who'd nicked who's sleeping bag. It was getting boring. I wanted out, so I started working on a nice new place with *TJ* and *Bill*.

***

One Sunday afternoon before I moved in, I was standing outside the concert venue with a few people when someone came by and told us that *Ash*, who thought she was *TJ*'s girlfriend, was getting hassled by the cops a little bit further down on Chalk Farm Road. I went down to see what was wrong, as I had gotten to fancy her a little bit by now.

The cops were trying to nick her 'cos some guy who owned a boutique there had seen her wearing a blue corduroy jacket, which he reckoned had been nicked from his shop a few weeks before. I had been given the jacket by some other guy. He hadn't said he'd nicked it, although I wouldn't have been surprised. He was an amphetamine dealer and he was always well dressed: nice leather jackets and boots, groovy shirts, suede or leather strides. I often sold speed for him, and I just thought the jacket was a bonus for doing a good job. I told the Old Bill that the jacket belonged to me, and that I had lent it to *Ash*, which was the truth, so they let her go and nicked me instead. They brought me down to the cop shop and charged me with dishonestly handling stolen goods. After they read me the charge and asked for a comment I said, 'Not Guilty.'

I had given my real name. I had never been busted in England before and I felt sure I was going to get off with this charge. I didn't know the jacket had been nicked, so I couldn't have dishonestly handled it. These were just my own thoughts about the whole thing but I did mention to the cops that I'd volunteered the information that it belonged to me, knowing that the Pakistani had said it was stolen from his shop, and I'd hardly have done that if I'd really dishonestly handled it.

It wasn't a major crime anyway, and the two coppers weren't really treating it as such, although a fence was seen in a worse light in the eyes of the law. I don't think they believed I was a major fence or anything. They knew I was just another long haired scraggy squatter, but the shop owner had made a complaint, and they were obliged to charge me with something. They didn't charge me with breaking into the place, as it probably would have involved more work. They did, however, ask me where I got the jacket, and rather than involve the guy who gave it to me, I told him I made it while working for my uncle, who was a tailor in Dublin. I gave them his name and number in case they needed confirmation.

The next morning I appeared in court, and was remanded in custody. I couldn't believe it. It was my first offence in England and a petty crime at that. The copper who nicked me had opposed bail on the grounds that I was Irish and of no fixed abode, and likely to leave the jurisdiction before the case came up. I hadn't given the squat as my permanent address for fear they might pay a visit. The whole community would probably have ended up getting nicked.

The remand was for two weeks, to Ashford, a remand centre for juveniles, as I was under 18 at the time. It was in Middlesex, near Heathrow Airport, miles away from London. Like in Ireland, people on remand could have a visit every day, but I knew I wouldn't be getting many. It would have been much easier if I'd been a few months older, and remanded to one of the adult prisons in the city itself.

It was my first time behind bars, and all the humiliation that went with it—strip search, insults, and commands. I was kicking myself that I hadn't pleaded guilty. I'd probably have been fined and out the same day. Why didn't they just nick me for some of the strokes I'd really pulled? I mean, I was dealing drugs, scamming people, picking pockets, robbing, and anything else I could to get together enough money for my next hit. I would have pleaded guilty straight away.

***

As I got deeper and deeper into heroin, I ended up staying off the streets by day and breaking and entering by night. *Willo* taught me this new trade, and we had many a scary moment together when we were convinced we'd be caught, and we were in no fit state to outrun anybody.

I was being driven on by an incessant hunger that just wouldn't go away. I craved heroin at every moment at this stage, needed to feel it flowing into my veins several times a day. My body was no longer trying to resist it; it had accepted its fate. I was now an out and out addict.

I was also an out and out criminal, because there was no other way of getting the cash I needed to spend on my daily addiction. The more heroin I took the more wasted I became, until I hardly knew what I was doing anymore. This, unsurprisingly, led to my being arrested several more times. On one particularly bad day I was charged with 'Attempting to steal amounts unknown from persons unknown,' which is a charge reserved for pickpockets.

This was on Portobello Road, and I was held in the cells over the long Easter weekend. When I appeared in court the following Tuesday I was granted bail, but was immediately re-arrested because they found out that there was a warrant out for me for 'taking pecuniary advantage', which is staying in a hotel without paying the bill. I didn't even remember that happening. I was shipped off to prison for a couple of weeks, and when a probation officer visited me he told me he would be recommending further imprisonment. He could see where I was heading with my life, and probably knew it would only be a matter of time before I turned up dead in an alley somewhere.

For some reason I was released from prison a few days before I was due to appear back in court, but somehow finding it in myself to realise my situation, I decided not to show up, and promptly returned to Ireland.

CHAPTER 8

When I got back to Ireland I pretty much just continued in the same vein, if you'll pardon the pun. I was living the life of a criminal, with no thought for the future or the past; just my present, and my need for heroin. I couldn't go very long without a hit, or I would start cramping up and would be hit by the sweats. When that happened, I was no good to anybody.

I reacquainted myself with all the guys I had known before I headed to London in 1969, and even though I had been away for nearly five years, it was as if I had just left the room and walked back in. Nothing had changed. Apart from the fact that some people were dead from overdoses or disease. I shrugged off these details because they meant nothing to me anymore.

All that mattered to me now was getting a regular fix of heroin, or whatever I could get my hands on, and I was using every trick in the book, and every little backstreet skill I had learned and perfected in London, in order to satisfy my craving.

I quickly went straight back into a routine of robbing and stealing, selling bum hash, doing dodgy cheques, and even breaking and entering in the chemists around the suburbs.

As soon as I managed to grab enough to score, I'd be straight off to the nearest dealer I knew, where I would waste no time in shooting up there and then. The rush would be over all too soon, and I'd have to go back out onto the streets, my gait getting slower and slower as I slipped into the nod, my eyelids barely open as I walked like a zombie around town, looking for my next chance to pounce on a bag, or a wallet.

I'd go for the chemists when there was a shortage of good gear around. I was too desperate at this stage to sit it out patiently. I needed a fix all the time, so I just had to go out and try to rob whatever I could use.

I was effectively homeless, because I was moving around from one hovel to another; wherever I was allowed to crash out after shooting up. I was always on the move anyway, constantly looking for my next fix.

I shudder at the thought of some of the places I must have ended up in at this stage in my life, and some of the people I had ended up with, but the memory is sometimes merciful, and this period is now, thankfully, more or less forgotten to me.

There are times when I get flashbacks of an image of my slumped body, draped over a chair, with a belt around my arm and a syringe sticking out of me, and I am not proud. But I know these would have been the more acceptable times, because I'm sure there was far worse that my mind now blocks out. It wasn't always possible to shoot up indoors, in the comfort of a safe house, and I'm sure I was not always that peaceful.

I can only imagine what kind of torture I put my family through at this time. It would have been common knowledge that I was a junkie, but I didn't care. I had managed to get myself away from everybody who loved me, and now I was on my own. The only thing I loved was heroin, and in my own mind, it was the only thing that cared for me. It was the only thing that made me feel good, even though it was making me feel so bad. I needed it, and I kept telling myself that I didn't need anything else.

Something had to give though. Deep in my mind I knew I wasn't really living. I kept hearing a nagging voice telling me to get out while I still could, but it was always too easily pushed back into the darkness. I knew I wasn't even enjoying the feeling of shooting up anymore. It had lost its power for me, because I had built up too much of a tolerance towards it, and even as I was feeding the stuff into a vein, I was thinking of having to go out and find some more money, dreading the thought of having to prowl the streets again, hoping I could make a quick snatch or maybe hook up with someone who had a few dodgy cheques to cash.

***

It was around this time when I was hanging around with *Martin*, and when we robbed that place out near Rathfarnham. When he got nicked but didn't grass me out, I knew I had been lucky. Other addicts with less of a sense of pride and honour would have sang to the gardaí if they were in his shoes that day. They'd have told them that I was the one behind the robbery and that they were only tagging along because they were sick; that they should let them go free and go after me instead.

Somehow, in a moment of clarity, I saw sense. I realised I wasn't exactly hanging around with the best sort of people, and that sooner or later I would end up serving some serious jail time. I knew I wouldn't be able for that, so there was only one other choice. I had to try to get clean and leave this lifestyle behind me.

It took a while to get myself together enough to actually do it, but I eventually managed to drag myself to a drugs clinic in Jervis Street, and told them I was an addict and wanted to get clean.

I was welcomed in like a sheep that had strayed from the flock and arrangements were made for me to go to St Loman's Psychiatric Hospital in Lucan on the border of Dublin.

My psychiatrist there was none other than Dr Noel Browne, the controversial doctor and politician. He interviewed me, asking if I really wanted to give up drugs, to which I replied that I did. He seemed satisfied with my answers and admitted me into the hospital's care.

I only spent about two weeks there in total—really only the beginnings of treatment, when I was at my weakest physically and mentally. They treated me as I suffered the excruciating withdrawal symptoms of intense pain, aching limbs, constant nausea and diarrhoea, but most of all they provided a place where I could not just get up and leave, and go looking for a fix to take all the pain away. It was a place of refuge for me in a time of need, but after the worst of the agony had passed, I realised that I no longer needed to stay there. I had admitted to myself that I was an addict, had heard myself say it, and had asked for help. I knew that I needed to get off heroin, and that was enough for me to know that I was capable of getting clean. My mind was still strong enough to tell me that much.

I decided to leave, and moved back into the family home with my ma. With a combination of her mothering me and my own will power, I managed to stay clean for the next five years.

It wasn't easy, and there were times when I just wanted to burst open the front door and go straight to the nearest dealer to get myself a nice big bag of scag, but I resisted the urge, and tried to keep myself busy, to keep my mind off it.

People I knew from outside the world of petty crime and junk saw what I was trying to do and supported me as much as they could. I was really touched by this, because I had made it as clear as day to everybody who came near me that I didn't need them, and didn't want them around me. Unless they were willing to 'lend' me some money.

One of my mates' fathers, a Garda Superintendent, knew all about me and had heard I was trying to go clean, and he went out of his way to organise a job as a storeman in a hardware wholesalers for me. He believed in second chances, and I jumped at it, knowing a full time job might keep me occupied enough to keep my mind off gear every second of the day. It didn't pay the earth but it was a job, and a helping hand at a time when I needed it most.

I stayed there for two years until I started selling life insurance. I'd gotten my feet out of the gutter and I was clean. I'd regained a lot of confidence in myself too, though at times I couldn't believe that I was now holding down a very respectable job, when only a couple of years before I had really been in the depths of despair and was going nowhere but to an early grave.

I discovered a natural flair for sales, and soon found myself with my own car. I stayed at home with my ma for the first couple of years because the money still wasn't great, but it was a step up from where I had been. This also made sure I wasn't open to too much temptation anymore, because I wasn't so sure I could trust myself without a sort of regime.

I kept active too, and regained my health, playing football and hurling with my brother's team, bringing back out all the skills I had abandoned. I was also pleased to be able to get back into a social scene—that had nothing to do with heroin—by hanging out with him and his mates, and heading to the pub with them every now and then. It stopped me from going up the walls, and I needed the distraction in those early times.

CHAPTER 9

Man, was I confused. I kept asking myself the same question: how the fuck did I end up here? Five years ago I had gone straight, kicked the habit, with no help from anybody, done the impossible, just cold turkey, and I hadn't touched anything for years.

I had gotten a job, a better job promotion in the better job, a driver's license, a car, a bigger car, a girlfriend, a beautiful girlfriend, the most beautiful girlfriend you could imagine. Things were on the up and up. I played soccer, hurling, football, golf. Shit, I was selling life insurance, advising people on their financial futures. Me, Shay, ex-junkie-turned-pillar-of-society. I'd cured myself and I also had the cure for the cure.

Her name was *Sarah*. She was beautiful, five-foot-seven, with full lips, and she was sweet 16. I saw her for the first time getting on a bus at the Halfway House and was smitten, but thought I'd never see her again. I was 23 and straight for the first time. I had just had my waist-length hair cut short and had started working, selling encyclopaedias door to door on a commission basis. I took to selling very well but the door-to-door part wore me out and I was between jobs when I saw her again.

My brother had brought me to a club in the city called Zhivago, one Saturday night. I was standing by the DJ booth trying to look smooth, as I wasn't yet comfortable with my smart new short-haired identity, when she sat beside me. I was really taken aback. When I had seen her get on the bus that day, I'd never expected to see her again, but now here she was, sitting right beside me in a crowded club. What should I do? I had no money to buy her a drink and I wasn't into asking chicks to dance, now that I was straight and still sober. I wasn't stoned and not exactly drunk either, as my brother's limited resources didn't really stretch to the shitty wines, for which the club charged £20 a bottle.

However, I felt this chance had been designed by the gods, so I took the bull by the horns and started to talk to her and within minutes we were getting on like a house on fire. I had expected the usual snub that came when you chatted up a particularly good-looking bird, and I wouldn't have minded too much if that had been the case. No one would have noticed, as she was sitting so close to me.

She was really friendly, as it turned out, and she was from the same suburb as me, Drimnagh. Within a few more minutes we were dancing and drinking wine, courtesy of her sister who worked in the club. She didn't mind that I had no money, which was even more of a surprise because with her looks she could attract millionaires. She was only 16 but could have passed for 18. She told me she was working for a cosmetics company in a big department store. I gave her insights into my background and told her I had been in London more or less all the time since I was 17. Loads of guys came and asked her to dance while we were chatting and she had refused them all, saying I was her boyfriend, although we weren't hugging or holding hands or anything.

It was magic, and the magic lasted all the way to Drimnagh as I walked her the five miles home, kissing and snogging along the way. I kissed her goodnight under the lamp post outside her house, got her phone number, and walked the rest of the way to my house with my head swirling. It had been so easy, but where would I get the money to ask her out again? One of the countless questions I was to ask myself about her over the next several years.

For our first date I finally got the money from my ma. She still believed in me getting a good education, and the week after I met *Sarah* coincided with enrolment in the night school. My ma gave me the money to enrol for five subjects for the Leaving Cert, as it would improve my job chances. I only enrolled for four and with the rest of the money I took *Sarah* to the Cherry Tree for a drink. From then on we were a couple.

Although we often argued and split up, we always got back together again. I was back to being a normal human being, playing football and hurling again, training twice a week and playing at the weekends, and the rest of the time meeting my bird. I had told her about the drugs and jail after I got to know her a bit better, and she didn't mind as long as I stayed off them. Life was perfect then.

***

Yeah … *Sarah*. Shit, I had memories of her. We had gone to London on holiday one year and I'd decided to visit *Aidan*, my old friend from Drimnagh, the one I had started out with on the long and sliding road, the one who was still strung out.

Over the four and a half years since I'd been with *Sarah*, I had met many an old junkie acquaintance in the pubs and clubs of Dublin and had never succumbed to the temptation to get stoned.

She knew about my past, and it was probably part of the fascination, the fact that I'd taken on and beaten the devil and she could live it all vicariously. She loved me to tell her about some of the crazy shit we got up to.

So there we were outside *Aidan*'s place. He and I had known each other for years and even though all the other guys in the gang had gotten stoned once or twice, only *Aidan* and I had made it a vocation.

He was living under a different name, an alias he had given to the cops the first time he was busted in London. Like most of us, he didn't want to get busted under his real name in case he ever did get it together to re-enter the real world.

I rang his bell a few times and there was no reply, but I was sure there was someone home. He was probably sleeping off a good stone. I knew he was a registered addict now and he was picking up a nice 'script' from the chemist every day. *Sarah* wanted to leave and check out the London she'd expected on her holiday; Buckingham Palace, Harrods and the like, but I convinced her to walk down to the school that I thought his kid might attend and, sure enough, around midday his girlfriend walked by on the opposite side.

'Hey,' I called.

She heard me but didn't immediately recognise me, as the last time she'd seen me I'd had really long hair.

'Shay, great to see ye, ye look great,' she said. '*Aidan* is just getting up. He'll be thrilled to see you. I'll collect the kid and go to the chemist and then we'll be off home.'

I introduced *Sarah* and, eventually, we made our way back to their apartment. Their kid, who was five, stayed outside to play and *Aidan*'s girlfriend went into the apartment first. It was on the first floor of a nice Edwardian house on a leafy road in Richmond, Surrey.

'*Aidan*, someone to see you.'

She didn't say who, keeping the element of surprise.

I walked in and he almost collapsed, looking at me as if a ghost had appeared.

'Wow, man, you look great, good to see you. I heard you're off the gear and doing great. What brings you back to London?'

'Uh well, I'm just over on holiday with *Sarah*, my girlfriend,' I said making the introductions. 'You look great yourself,' I lied.

He looked like shit, with teeth missing from a set that used to be perfect, hair still long but with scraggy split ends—his major fear as a teenager. I mean, he used to iron his wranglers. The five years he'd continued shooting up while I was off had taken their toll. Looking around, I could see that they were trying to maintain something resembling a respectable life, with the kid and the various personal touches they had brought to the room, but you only had to look at *Aidan* to know that a junkie lived here.

The atmosphere was strained. I didn't have the small talk to bridge the last five years. I couldn't talk about his family, as none of them had spoken to me since I'd arrived back in Dublin; I didn't know any dealers we could discuss; I wasn't sick, I didn't have an abscess or a favourite doctor;

I wasn't robbing or stroking, no one I knew was in the nick. I was lost for a subject.

'Sit down, *Sarah*,' *Aidan*'s girlfriend said, 'I'll make a cup of tea.'

She handed *Aidan* the bag she had collected from the chemist, and then he found the words I'd been secretly longing to hear for the past few years, 'Do you fancy a turn-on Shay?'

I didn't dive straight in. I'd been in this situation loads of times since I'd been straight and had always said no, but this was different. I'd always felt guilty about leaving *Aidan* behind, still strung out in London, and I always felt bad every time I saw his parents. They were probably thinking, there I was leading a normal life, having led their son astray and then left him behind in London, addicted; a junkie.

I'd always wanted a chance to get him back on the straight and narrow. Seeing him now though, in the state he was in, I knew there was no chance he was going to be like me, straight, going out with the girl next door as it were, leading the life we had consciously rejected years before. We'd never intended going down that road, saving for a house, getting married, having kids. No, we were gonna change the world, we were gonna be free, and we were gonna die young. I felt like a traitor to the cause. The song, 'Almost Cut My Hair' was swirling around my head for some reason.

I looked to *Sarah* for approval. She was 20 now, a young woman, and I sought her approval first.

'It's up to you, I've no problem with it,' she said.

Most people would probably have detected the note of disapproval in those words, the disappointment, worry, and possibly even a little sadness, but my mind wasn't open to such things. All I was hearing were the words that said I could go right ahead.

Approval obtained, I think I was saying thanks as *Aidan* handed me a syringe and a half a grain of pure National Health heroin.

Sarah asked if she could look, out of curiosity—regardless of her disapproval, she did still find my darker side interesting—and watched as I got a fix together. I dissolved the NHS heroin onto the spoon, then mopping it with some cotton wool, I sucked it into the syringe. After a few years off it, my veins had recovered somewhat, so I had no trouble finding one, and with my mind focused on one thing and one thing only—the intense expectation of the immense rush I was about to feel—I slid the needle into my arm and unleashed that devil once again upon myself. The feeling was one of sheer bliss, and I couldn't believe I had gone so long without it. It was like feeling the most beautiful sensation rippling through every fibre of my body, sheer ecstasy washing over me, and when the rush subsided and a warm, soft wave of pleasure, leaving me halfway between wake and sleep but still fully aware of just how good I felt, I knew that *Aidan* and I finally had something to talk about: our self-destruction.

***

The rest of our holiday was a disaster, with arguments and recriminations, and everywhere I took her I was secretly hoping to meet someone I knew with a bit of scag so I could just forget all the shit.

'I'm not strung out,' I kept telling her, 'I'm just having a couple of turn-ons for old time's sake. I'll be OK when I get back to Dublin, I'm on my holidays.'

But something was lost between us that day in *Aidan*'s apartment, which would never come back. The respect she'd had for me, for the strength she thought I had, was gone; she couldn't trust me anymore, and it had nothing to do with sex or a wayward eye. She couldn't trust me to be straight. She told me she wanted to split up.

What should have been a holiday to cement our relationship became an unmitigated disaster. I went back to work selling insurance when I got home but my heart wasn't in it anymore. My heart was with *Sarah*, but her heart was not with mine. My work suffered badly and the skills I had used to get me sent on an advanced sales course to London in record time seemed to have abandoned me. So did my will to work, and after a while it was just so much easier to say, 'You know what? Fuck it,' and take a few more hits for old time's sake.

I tried telling her that I wasn't back on gear, but it was obvious that I was, and she stopped meeting me. Pretty soon she stopped answering the phone. She knew my recent behaviour, my elusiveness and my change in appearance meant only one thing, but I was denying everything.

The final straw came when she got confirmation of all she had suspected.

I got busted one night for possession, and was remanded in custody. I got two weeks in Mountjoy, and on the first night I walked in, I looked up, and who did I see only her brother-in-law, who was a prison officer there. I'd say he was on the phone to her that very night.

For her, there was no going back. I knew there would be no way back for me either, if I didn't sort myself out, and soon.

One day, after a particularly nasty argument, I saw an ad in the paper: 'Salesmen wanted in Germany'. That was it! I could take a 'Geographical cure' and get as far away from every dealer I knew as possible. I went for the interview, got the job, sold my car, said my goodbyes, and I was gone within a couple of weeks. Another chapter, I thought. A new start; get away from it all.

***

A couple of weeks before I left for Germany though, I was introduced to a nice looking blonde chick in Davy Byrnes in Duke Street, which was an upmarket watering hole at that time. She was tall and blonde, a little bit on the heavy side, and she was from one of the most expensive places to live in South Dublin. It was only a couple of days since I'd split with *Sarah*, and this girl had all the right credentials to replace her in my heart. When I asked her why she was limping, and she told me she'd crashed her motorcycle sidecar at the races in the Phoenix Park that day. I was impressed enough to make a play and, surprisingly, it worked.

We had a lot in common. She had just split with her racing driver boyfriend, although I didn't know it at the time; she didn't know that I'd just split with *Sarah* either, but we both had the same motivation. We gave ourselves to each other out of a need for revenge and, while I tried to avoid her bruises on that first night together, during the next fortnight I added some more. It was a bruising two weeks. We paraded ourselves as totally in love in her old boyfriend's local, and then again in *Sarah*'s local, and by the time I left for Germany, there were bruised egos and bruised hearts, but the real bleeding was about to begin, for me.

In all the passion I succumbed to the needle once again—just a couple of turn-ons before I left—and remember vividly when the Pope visited Dublin in 1979. I spent the visit watching him on TV in a flat in Rathmines. He was saying mass for 500,000 people. I was stoned out of my head and wondering whether he and his audience knew what they were missing—The Peace, *Requiescant in Pace*.

***

The job in Germany proved almost as interesting as the interview I'd attended in the Shelbourne Hotel a few weeks earlier. I had gone dressed in my life insurance uniform: shirt, tie and the works. When I got to the room in the hotel there was no one there; no applicants, no interviewer; it was a very hot day so I sort of understood why there were no applicants, but the lack of an interviewer was a new one on me.

I, however, was on a mission. I'd just parted from *Sarah* and because my fling straight afterwards failed to arouse any jealousy in her, I told myself I needed to be gone quickly so she'd realise how much she missed my presence. But no interviewer—it was weird. Finally this little guy arrived in the room and said, 'Hi, how *are* ya?' I could hear he was American.

'Good,' I said, and waited. He drifted towards the window and seemed to get lost in his thoughts, looking out on St Stephen's Green.

I waited some more and after a while he said, 'Do you like sex?'

'Yeah,' I replied, 'but with women…' (In case he got the wrong impression.)

'Do you like a drink?'

'Yeah,' I replied, 'I enjoy a drink.'

'And a smoke?'

'Yeah, I enjoy a smoke … cigarettes, I mean.'

'Then you're going to enjoy this job,' he said, like I'd already passed the test.

He wasn't joking; it was a relief to leave this new girl behind and more of a relief to leave the dope behind. I'd begun lying to myself and I'd been scoring every chance I got. Germany was going to rid me of temptation for one simple reason; I wouldn't know where to score.

CHAPTER 10

I was met by *Guy* at Frankfurt Airport. He was driving a seven series BMW; a little culchie in a nice jam jar. I was impressed; he must have been doing something right. It took us a couple of hours to reach the small village in Bavaria that was to be our HQ. After a few days getting acclimatised and meeting the locals we set out to work. I learned that my job was to visit the American bases around Germany and sell fine bone china tea services to GIs stationed there. I didn't care. I just needed to take my mind off heroin and make sure I was too busy to start making new contacts who could get me some.

I was going through some bad withdrawals, but it was made a little bit easier knowing that there was just no way I could score. Unlike at home, when I'd try to lock myself up and fight the urge to go out and buy some nice scag, saying 'Fuck all that' to my pathetic attempts to stay clean by giving in as soon as it got hard, there was nothing I could do here. I had no idea where to buy drugs, where the dealers hung out, nothing. For me, there simply were no drugs to be had, so I had better just get over it and move on.

Even though I knew this wasn't strictly true, I managed to convince myself that it was, and got through cold turkey by keeping myself busy and battling my demons at night. Some nights were harder than others, but I managed to get through it.

***

We visited several bases in the first few days. We would drive up to the gate and show our ID card and, having been allowed in, we'd set up our stall and just start talking to the soldiers.

The first couple of times I just listened to my new colleagues give their pitch. 'Hey Joe, have you had a chance to check out our program?'

'No I don't think so.'

'Let me tell you about it. This is the fine bone china program for Mother's Day. It's a program which allows you the opportunity to reserve one of our exclusive fine bone china tea services to send home to your mother for Mother's Day. Wouldn't that be nice?'

'Yeah!'

'Let me show you how it works.'

I listened to them all, saying the same things, asking the same questions, hearing the same answers: 'Yeah, good idea.' 'How does it work?' 'Where do I sign?'

It was a piece of piss—much easier than selling life insurance. I took to it like a duck to water.

On our second day, I'd already learned a lot: Don't talk to anyone with a high rank. Don't talk to Military Policemen.

'Why not?' I had to ask.

'Just don't. There's enough customers out there. We don't need them.'

On my second day one of the MPs asked us for our clearance to sell on the base. I saw *Guy* show him some papers but the MP wasn't satisfied and told us to pack up our display. He took our gear and put it in his car and told us to follow him to the MP station. After about two hours filling out all sorts of papers, they were accusing us of trespassing and selling illegally on the base, but having determined that we were beyond their jurisdiction, being Irish, they called the German Police. The German police established that we'd been invited onto the base, having shown our ID cards, and so let us go. It was too late when we left the MP station to go back to work. The MPs kept our ID cards, accompanied us off the base, and we drove away.

The others, all experienced hands, looked to see my reaction and, discovering that I wasn't bothered, set off with me to find a hotel, drink a few beers and set about making some new ID cards. It was there that they filled me in on the whole set-up. I wasn't sure if they expected me to react in some way, maybe with shock or horror, but to be honest I was amazed, and admired the simplicity of such a neat scam. I had done much worse back home, so there were no moral dilemmas for me here.

We were selling the 21-piece tea services for $799. They cost no more than $30 from Beleek, including post and packaging. The soldiers had up to two years to pay. We just got them to sign a contract and a postcard to their mother or wife to say the set had been ordered and would arrive within six to eight weeks. If they had second thoughts after we left, they'd think about the postcard we sent to their loved ones on their behalf, and think three times—very thoughtful of us.

The whole scam had been dreamed up by an Irish guy. He was a Kildare man, the others told me, and from a very poor background, but now he was a millionaire and was able to indulge in some expensive hobbies like polo and opening restaurants.

For me it was a handy way of making money, hassle free, and it took my mind off the gear. I was busy all day trying to flog tea sets to US soldiers, and in the evenings I was busy familiarising myself with my new surroundings, getting used to the foreign sights and sounds. There was also quite a social scene, with several bars playing good music every night, and this and a few drinks every night helped me to stay away from giving in to the urge and going out searching the streets for dealers.

After three months, in the run up to Christmas 1979, I felt I had stayed away long enough to rid my body of the heroin that had tried to overtake it, and more importantly, the urge to take it again. I was also getting a little bit tired of the situation in Germany, where the novelty of my new surroundings was beginning to wear off. I had saved enough money to arrive home with some pride, so I decided to return to Dublin and to my ma's house.

I hoped I could pick up where I had left off before I had fallen back into the heroin trap that time in London, that I could find a decent job, maybe even win *Sarah* back. But even the best laid plans can sometimes fall apart, and things didn't work out the way I wanted them to.

Chapter 11

After being off drugs, clean, for nearly five years, with a little relapse followed by another year clean after *Sarah* broke up with me, I was pretty confident that that was that. I was rid of addiction. But all it took was one spark of a suggestion, one chance, and I would be back on the gear. That's how it turned out for me, but it's not like I was the only one. *Terry* had just come off a rehab course and was claiming to be clean for a while when I met him in my local pub one night.

I had been on my way to work; a night shift in the tyre factory. He told me how he was going to stay clean and all he needed was a job and everything would be hunky-dory. I was staying clean, having realised my mistake, so I knew how *Terry* felt and I told him I'd see if I could fix him up with a job in the same factory as me.

A couple of days later I was able, through an old girlfriend of mine who worked in personnel, to get him hooked up. She organised it so that we were both on the same shift, where we could lend each other moral support.

After about six weeks of changing shifts and about £100 a week cash-in-hand, *Terry* and I got on the number 18 bus to head for the night shift.

We had our customary few pints to get the buzz on, which would help take us through to 7am, when he sprung it on me.

'Do you know what I did earlier tonight?'

'No,' I replied

'I broke into the pharmacy in Our Lady's Hospital for Sick Children.'

'What!'

I was shocked, not just because of what he said, but because my younger sister worked there. Instead of telling him what a cunt he was for doing such a thing, and that he was supposed to be going straight, I found myself saying, 'What did you get?'

'About 3,000 amps of morphine. Do you fancy a turn-on?'

I don't know what made me say yes. A combination of things, I suppose. I still wasn't over the split with *Sarah*, I was working in a factory, life was a total drag. I'd come back down in the world, having been a successful salesman earning good money and driving a nice car, to working the night shift in a factory. The last few months had been bad for my ego. Whatever it was, we were off the bus and heading back to *Terry*'s house to dig up the stash in his back garden and get stoned. 3,000 amps of morphine—it seemed like a lifetime's supply!

It was gone in six weeks. We weren't going to keep this habit going on £100 a week, so we both knew we had to get back into the junkie lifestyle and find money some other way. From there, my life turned back into a nightmare.

I was strung out again, spending every day looking for cash, scoring, shooting up, then looking for more heroin, almost as soon as the first rush had worn off. Once again, my tolerance went right back up to where it used to be, and I found myself having to take more and more just to get the desired effect. After a while, I found myself having to use a serious amount just to feel 'normal' and not suffer any of the unpleasant withdrawal symptoms. It got to the stage where I wasn't even enjoying it any more, because I knew that as soon as I'd cooked up what I had, I would immediately have to go back out and get some more money to do it all over again. It was a hand to mouth existence.

It wasn't long before I was thrown out of my home. Or maybe I just left. Either way, I ended up sleeping in various squats, flats and hovels—wherever the drugs were.

I hadn't managed to get my own pad together since I went back on it and it was a godsend when *Jackie*, who was the sister of a major dealer, told me I could stay in her spare room when it suited me.

It was a really nice apartment in South Dublin; a mews maisonette with a lot of quaint decoration on the outside. *Jackie's* family were one of the main movers in the drug scene in Dublin and the first of the heavy gangs to get involved in drugs. They were one of those amazing Dublin families; lots of kids, all reared for villainy of some sort, and all with their own area of expertise—banks and post offices, protection and kidnapping, and so on. No one in the family was straight as far as I knew.

This meant that not only did I get a lot of good quality gear for free, or discount prices, but I was also rubbing shoulders with some seriously dodgy people. Of course, as a result, I was also being watched by the cops.

***

God, I've been here for ages. I don't know why I didn't leave hours ago. It's really silent now after all the screaming that was going on earlier. Nobody's said anything to me since the guy who was checking on me asked me if I wanted anything to eat.

I had to say no to the food 'cos my stomach was starting to heave. I hadn't gone that long without a turn-on for over 18 months, except for the couple of times when I got nicked.

I never ate a lot when I was on the gear anyway, but that was 'cos I never felt hungry when I was stoned. The gear itself was like eating and drinking. Now it was wearing off, and even though I hadn't eaten all day, I still couldn't dream of eating a thing. The way my stomach was churning, I knew I'd just throw up. I knew soon I was going to have terrible cramps and shivers, and I was getting anxious about everything. The thought of doing a runner came back into my head, but I was caught in an internal debate over what to do.

It must be midnight already. The last bus into town must be already gone, and I've no money for a taxi and no way of knowing if Jodie would be home to pay the fare.

It was as silent as a morgue now in the place. Surely to God it was too late for an interview. I started thinking that maybe they'd arrange for me to be brought to the detox in Jervis Street and have me come back some other day. Jesus, I would have done anything for a turn-on at that very minute, just to forget about all the shit.

I started to think that maybe I should just get up and go home to my ma's and do a cold turkey, and just stay off like I'd done before. I had to ask myself: Would she let me in though?

I'd tried that route the previous Christmas. I got a script for 50 Diaconal from the doctor during Christmas week. I went home on Christmas Eve and my plan was to take no more than three a day for as long as they lasted, and then just kick it. I couldn't keep to my limit though, and they were all gone by New Year's Eve. There was a really nice hit off Dike, better than smack even, but as they came in tablet form, as a painkiller for cancer patients, you had to crush them up first. There was always the danger of the blood clotting if you couldn't get a good hit, which was always a danger in my case as I had hardly any good veins left.

No, I knew I had to stay at the Lodge, because the main reason I was telling myself I was there was to stay out of jail. I was shitting myself with worry about my court case. I had to get into rehab to avoid a long jail sentence, but it was starting to dawn on me, ever so slightly, that my going through the motions might not be enough. I would need to mean it this time. I would have to actually try to stay off drugs for good. I wasn't a kid any more. I didn't know what was going to happen in court, but I knew they wouldn't just take my word for it that I was clean and going to be a good boy from here on in.

As far as the drug squad was concerned, I was one of the leading lights in the mob, by association. As I hung around with major criminals, it was an easy conclusion to draw, and it would be easy to put across to the judge the role they felt I was playing in this criminal family. Catching me in possession of some high quality heroin was inevitable, and when they did, they threw in cheque fraud for good measure. They knew exactly what I had been up to. I was sure to get 14 years or more.

God! That would mean I wouldn't be out until I was at least 40. They'd never accept the plea that I was a victim in this whole thing; a junkie like all the thousands of other junkies out there, probably worse off than most of them, as I'd been on it longer than most of the people they were writing about in the papers every day. From Fatima Mansions, Dolphin House, St Theresa's Gardens and every other block of corporation flats from Sallynoggin to Ballymun and all the posh houses in between.

The publicity this shit had been getting in the last year was unreal, and this was my main problem. They were writing about it as if heroin addiction in Dublin had just started 12 months before. There seemed to be a widely held belief that the heroin epidemic had started and was centred around the Sheriff Street area of the inner city, but I remember scoring smack as far back as 1969.

Admittedly, there weren't many of us back then, maybe a core group of 50. In fact, if the cops had been doing their job back then, they could have nipped the whole thing in the bud. But as far as I was concerned, they had a vested interest in keeping us on the streets 'cos without junkies there was no need for a drugs squad. *Maybe I could bring that theory up in court by way of mitigation:*

'Your honour, I'm here today because the drugs squad made sure that I'd remain a junkie, back in the 1960s when there weren't enough of us around, so that they'd still have a job while they were waiting for it to turn into an epidemic. I further contend your honour, that they ignored the obvious signs of the beginning of an epidemic and the entry of organised crime into the Dublin drug scene, by allowing gangs to organise without any fear of being busted, until they had grown into a full blown Mafia, and now that they've succeeded in creating this monster, they're trying to allay some of the bad publicity they're getting by busting a few junkies like me.'

Of course, that was just my junkie logic at work.

We had to go out and rob every day for our gear, and being experienced old hands just meant we needed more money for more dope than the average new arrival on the scene. It was around this time that I started doing the cheque books and bank cards with *Podge* and at times I was getting a good bit of money in. It would all go on heroin straight away, but that didn't matter to me.

The thing was that now, unlike years before when we had been forced to break into chemists and get whatever drugs we could find, now the streets of Dublin were awash with gear. It was everywhere, which is why the newspapers were all over it, and why the police were cracking down, and watching the likes of me.

We acted like we didn't have a care in the world, and didn't give a fuck about anybody or anything, but that wasn't strictly true. We lived in fear. There was the fear of being busted, which we all knew was inevitable at some stage, due to the sheer amount of criminal offences we were committing every single day. There was the fear of being busted straight after scoring gear. And then of course there was the fear of not being able to score at all.

For *Deano,* having a close friend in the hierarchy didn't mean anything more than us knowing the best places to score; and the dope we were buying had a higher purity than what the average junkie had to buy in the street. All this meant was that we were more addicted than the rest of them. Most of the time, we had to pay like everyone else.

Sure, there were a few extra perks, as it were. Sometimes we'd get invited to some of the clubs in town when these guys and other kingpins would be having a night out to celebrate some particularly lucrative deal, and were lashing out a few quid while hobnobbing with the stars of the day—but that was about it. We might get the odd gram thrown in if we managed to put them on to a good deal.

It was totally unreal. I was baffled by the fact that the top guys hadn't been busted. One of them lived close to the cop shop in Sundrive Road. Kilos were moved through there on a weekly basis and it wasn't like they tried to hide it. I was so sure there was going to be a big bust there some day that I used to avoid going there when I knew there was a lot of gear knocking about.

I remember one night when I made an exception. I had met Philo and one of his mates in the Bailey; Philo and his new band Thin Lizzy had just finished a tour. Normally I'd just nod and not get involved with all the hangers-on and groupies that'd be hanging around with them, but Philo himself came over to me and asked me if I had any gear. I hadn't, but I knew that my dealer was expecting a delivery that night. So we headed up towards his place. We stopped at a chipper in Cork Street on the way up 'cos another guy, who had invited himself, was hungry. It was obvious that the gear had successfully arrived as there were kids outside the chipper asking us if we wanted to score; ten and 11 years old. Some of them were using already.

When we arrived at the house, I knew we were in luck as there were a few nice cars parked outside—the inner circle had assembled. The dealer's car was there. He actually knew Philo well over the years and I knew there'd be no objection to us being there as they always liked to have famous people around. There were always a few of those who were in need of their services.

There were all sorts of hoods there, from all walks of crime. My dealer's brother and his partner, armed robbers, were there, as well as his oldest brother, a jack of all trades learned since childhood during his apprenticeships in Daingean and Letterfrack reform schools, while under the supervision of the Christian Brothers.

He used to tell me stories about these places which were unreal; how they were treated, how much they were battered, starved and enslaved, working in the fields as farmers. The graduates of these institutions made up most of the crime bosses of Dublin. All the friendships and criminal alliances had been forged there many years earlier.

The guy who had invited himself along was flabbergasted as he sat down. The papers were writing every day about the war on drugs, and here we were, 500 yards from the police station, with every major player in the drug scene, and kilos of the stuff getting shared out. If the house had been busted that night they could have sorted out 90% of the city's drug problem in one fell swoop. But the Gardaí were probably patrolling the flats, busting some poor junkie with a few packs for possession with intent to supply.

Those junkies were unlikely to pull out a piece and blow your head or your balls off, as one of the armed robbers sitting amongst us actually had. They were hardly likely to be volunteering to enter this gaff on this particular evening.

Philo was just delighted to be there, and was more than happy to have a smoke with the boys, chasing the dragon without a care in the world. He wasn't as freaked as I thought he would be, but then again he had often been with the boys in the clubs in Leeson Street, into the early hours; and being in the rock business, he was used to being around loads of gear. Being famous, of course, Philo didn't have to do anything to attract people or drugs, he was like a magnet, and I even got a free matchbox full for bringing the famous personages along. I suppose it was these little things which made me acceptable and trusted by the powers that be.

**

Another night *Deano* and I got a tip off that there was a lot of scag in town. It had been brought in by an independent—a student in UCD who was strung out, and some Turkish guy. The guy who gave us the tip off was a posh junkie who owed some money to one of the dealers, and he was hoping that *Deano* might put a good word in or help him out if things got on top.

We made contact with the student and told him we were interested in buying all the gear, and he introduced us to the Turk. We hadn't any money of course but we knew where he could offload whatever he had, and we were hoping to make a few grams of commission from the deal. We brought the Turk back to this guy *Obi's* apartment and he brought a sample for us to taste. It was beautiful uncut rocks, and he had a few kilos to move.

Suitably impressed with the goods, we made a few phone calls while the Turkish guy was watching TV and drinking a cup of tea. *Deano* finally contacted *Shammy*, who said he was interested and would be by in an hour. He arrived within the hour with another guy, and I nearly died when he walked in the door, 'cos this guy was a lunatic, and he and I weren't seeing eye to eye over a car deal. He reckoned I still owed him a few bob.

They said hello to *Deano* and the other guy just grunted in my direction. I hadn't known that he and *Shammy* were partners. For the moment, any disputes were set aside 'cos of the business at hand. *Deano* was about to introduce them to the Turk, who had just turned to greet them, when *Shammy* dived on him and grabbed him by the throat, saying, 'You, you fuckin bollix. You ripped me off in Istanbul last year. You owe me 20 grand and I want it back.'

Then, turning to the other guy, he said, 'Get himself on the phone and tell him to get down here straight away.'

He got on the horn and made the call as ordered.

Me and *Deano* were as shocked as the Turk, whose tan had quickly disappeared. *Shammy* told us he had been in Turkey the year before and that this guy was the one who had ripped him off for £20,000. It was hard enough to believe that *Shammy* could get ripped off anywhere, and even if he had been, the likelihood that this was the same guy was very slim indeed. We didn't try to defend the Turk; we knew *Shammy* wanted whatever gear he had, and wanted to let him know that he didn't appreciate the incursion onto his turf.

Deano, in the few minutes we had before the others arrived, was now negotiating with *Shammy* for our commission 'cos he knew the ownership had just changed hands. He was promised a good turn-on by *Shammy*, and when the others arrived a few minutes later they bundled the Turk into the car and left.

A few hours later, one of the guys came back and told us the Turk had gotten away. It was hard to believe. It didn't take a genius to figure out the Turk was not going to be seen again. But to make it more credible, he didn't have a turn-on for us.

CHAPTER 12

It was during this time that I met my saviour from Fatima Mansions, the woman who threatened to jump out a window in order to save me from being murdered: *Jodie*. She christened herself with a new name when she left the orphanage up North and moved to Dublin.

I don't know why she was never adopted; she was too good looking to be a brasser, if that's possible. I never did ask her why she was never adopted. It was bad enough to be dropped off at the orphanage as a little kid and then be rejected by every potential foster parent for 15 years when all your mates were being taken to new homes to get new names and were never to be seen again. Maybe the nuns wanted to keep her, to bring her up to lead the life they'd forsaken—reared by the nuns in the North to become a brasser in Dublin.

I met her in a pub in Rathmines. I was feeling really good. I'd been out dipping, or picking pockets and bags, with *Deano*, who was easily one of the best in the business. Even by his standards we got lucky and we'd touched for a few grand in our first dip of the day. We'd enough money to keep our habits going and were going to take a few days off—no sense in tempting fate. We were on our holidays now, we decided, and we'd only touch for something now if it came up and bit us on the nose.

Three and a half grand was a nice touch in our business; no violence, no alarms, just nifty fingers and a disappearance act, grab a taxi and back to the gaff. We were going to score a bit of coke as well; tonight would be a Horse and Charlie night. We were going to go looking for a bird, like normal human beings, not just shooting up smack and goofing off, watching the telly or reading the newspapers. We were going out on the town. It was going to be magic.

We went back to my gaff; the place where I was staying with *Jackie*. I couldn't just bring any person back, because technically I wasn't even living there, and I had to mind my Ps and Qs a little. If I had started bringing back every junkie who wanted somewhere warm and dry to shoot up, I'd have been out on my ear before I knew what hit me.

Jackie called in our order and me and *Deano* began the ritual of getting our veins up, a ritual he and I had been through many times together since the late 1960s in Dublin and London. A lot of collapsed veins were the result and we had to look long and hard to find the right one. We were sitting with our feet in basins of hot water when *Dave* arrived with the gear. He was a motorcycle courier who worked for one of the dealers and he guaranteed delivery of big amounts within half an hour. Sort of like Pizza Hut.

We had ordered an ounce of scag, 28 grams, and two grams of coke for £1,700. Normally we'd use a gram a day at £100 a gram, so it was a nice deal for us; half price and better quality because we were on the fringes of the hierarchy.

We had a couple of nice shots of smack and coke—speedballs we called them—a rare treat. We followed this up with a few lines of coke, which we did with *Jackie* and *Yvette*, who weren't junkies but liked a turn-on every now and then. It was perfect. There was no paranoia from the coke that couldn't be cured by a nice hit of smack, it was just pure electric exhilaration and confidence.

***

I was exuding confidence when I met *Jodie* later on in the pub. It was a packed Thursday night payday—the start of the weekend in Dublin. The 'cosiest' pub in Rathmines at the end of a 'cosy' day, no hanging around waiting to score, no sneaking into the jacks for a fix, just a normal night out on the razzle.

As soon as she walked in I knew she was the one. That's why I loved coke; no shyness, no fear of rejection, nothing could possibly go wrong. She was beautiful, with straight, shiny black hair, a middle parting on top but with a fringe, and the rest falling around her face. She looked real 1960s.

A few pints, a few furtive snorts for me, a few Carlsberg Specials for *Jodie*, and a half an hour after closing time, I was in her bed in her apartment, having arranged with *Deano* to collect me there in the morning.

We had sex all night long, as I couldn't orgasm because of all the gear inside me. She thought I wasn't climaxing because I wasn't enjoying myself, but nothing could have been further from the truth. I didn't want to tell her the real reason, as she didn't know I was a junkie. In what seemed like a fair deal, I didn't know she was a hooker.

I calmed her fears about her performance and reassured her that things would be different the next day. I nodded off to sleep eventually, enveloped in her arms. I hadn't been with a woman since I went back on the gear full time, and it was a beautiful feeling after such a long time.

I made it with her again the next morning before I got stoned, and climaxed within a couple of minutes; this reassured her that she was all woman. Afterwards, while she was having a bath I got a turn-on together and got stoned again. *Deano* called down later as promised, and we split up the gear and the rest of the poke, promising to meet again in a few days to go out working before it all ran out.

I just sorted of drifted into living with *Jodie* after that. As we got to know and trust each other better, I told her I was a junkie and she told me she was a brasser. I think we both suspected anyway. These were details that were a little difficult to keep from your lover.

I never intended it to be the way it was, with *Jodie* giving me money, but I had to admit I felt I was onto a sweet deal. It relieved some of the pressure of having to constantly go out robbing, because even though I still went out with *Deano* most days, I had the safety net of knowing that if I returned home empty handed, she would give me the money to score enough to get me by. Usually enough to get me by that night and then the next morning. I never had to ask her; it was just understood, and I was in no situation to start queering the deal by asking for reasons.

It wasn't long before we had become business partners because, by the time the bread and the dope ran out, I had lost contact with *Deano* and she was my only source of income.

We had a bit of an unholy pact going. She was giving me enough money to score, while I became her *raison d'etre*, someone to mother, a substitute for the kid she'd aborted in order to go on working and guarantee the income that she was now giving to me, her adult child.

I don't know what I gave her in return for her kindness. After a while I wouldn't even give her a ride. She'd come home from work, after riding some judge or priest on the canal by Fitzwilliam Square, wake me up from a serious goof and beg me to give her one. Most nights I told her to fuck off, but sometimes I had to, in order to ensure the continuous flow of shekels. Her income was steadier than mine because there were plenty of dirty fuckers around.

I didn't consider myself a pimp or anything. A pimp was something different, and they just took bread off the chicks and bought flashy cars and suits and were really heavy and beat the chicks up. I didn't do any of that shit. I just wanted to get stoned, and if *Jodie* wanted to throw her hard earned money at me, expecting nothing in return, so be it. For me, it was a marriage made in heaven.

Adieu, *Jodie*, abandoned once again in the clinic in Jervis Street hospital.

***

I have to get off this bench and tell her I'm sorry. I didn't mean to leave you, please forgive me, I don't want to save myself, I swear. I swear on my ma's life I don't. Mary, mother of God, please believe me.

I was suddenly filled with an overwhelming urge to get off that bench. I told myself that I never felt like I needed to be saved. I never felt I was dying, suffocating, hyperventilating. I didn't need a doctor or a nurse or an oxygen tent. I didn't need a saviour. I didn't need help.

Help for what? Saved from what? Saving was putting something by for the future so you could have security in your old age. I definitely didn't need security. I didn't have enough money to need security. Security was for banks, big estates, walls, prisons, bars, chains. I wanted to be insecure, free, no guarantees, without focus, blurred, constantly in a state of flux, hanging suspended between life and death: almost dead—surrounded by love, being touched with baby touches, being talked about and whispered to by people who'd forgotten all my failures, foibles and weaknesses, drifting between life and death, goofing off, bringing tears to the eyes of loved ones, then waking up. Life, death and resurrection, constant flux, rapid eye movement, occupying the space between God and Man, the infinite space, no beginning, no end, explicable only in monetary terms, the ultimate product, the killer of all pain, entry into the space ... I NEED HELP!

***

I screamed it this time, just like they asked. I wasn't sure I meant it but I was shaking when I said it. I didn't want to sit on the bench any more and think about my life. It seemed like someone else's life, the more I thought about it. Whoever it was that was living, it wasn't me. I was shaking and just about to cry. The tears were welling up in my eyes when all the interviewers stood up from the circle they had been sitting in, walked over, and gave me a hug. 'Welcome to Coolmine,' they all said, as they put their arms around me.

That was it. That what was what I'd been afraid of, I was thinking, as the tears disappeared from my eyes. I was introduced to this guy who I vaguely remembered, and he showed me to my room. There were three sets of bunk beds. It was already 3am and he told me the wake up call would be at 7am.

I was glad to hear that. I felt like I'd lived a couple of lifetimes on the bench, and despite the relief I'd felt having screamed for help, and being hugged for my trouble, I knew from experience that I wouldn't be going asleep any time soon. This guy was whispering 'cos everybody who hadn't been sitting up waiting for me to cave in was asleep. That surprised me, as these were the same people who had been screaming and roaring at each other a few hours earlier. He seemed to pick up on my fears and he brought me back out into the hall to show me his room, which was just a few doors down. He told me if I needed anything or if I couldn't sleep, I should just call him; and with that, I sneaked into my bed.

The wake up call came at 7am sharp. I hadn't slept a wink but the others, who had all been fast asleep, jumped out of bed at the first call and immediately started to make their beds. One of them showed me the standard which was expected, and was regimental. I'd been tossing and turning all night so my bed was in a heap. I managed to tuck it and fold like he explained, and having dressed and washed, we headed down for breakfast; cornflakes, a big fry, and tea.

Anyone else would probably look forward to that, almost tasting it before they even sat down, and if I'd been myself I probably would have too. But I wasn't really myself; I was a heroin addict—a bad one—so I couldn't even look at the food, and just sipped on the tea instead, concentrating hard on not throwing up. I was sitting beside a small dark haired bird from Phibsboro whom I'd never met before, and she was giving me a quick surmisal of how things worked in the Lodge. At 8am the bell was rung and everybody brought their dishes out to the kitchen. Then we headed for the big room where I had been interviewed. The bell ringer called it The Group Room.

The seats had been rearranged around the perimeter of the room, not like when I had stood against the wall facing eight people on chairs in the middle of the room. It was a fairly big sitting room with big French windows and the seating was a mixture of sofas, armchairs and hard chairs. I found a seat and everybody was chatting away until *Kieran* came in and introduced himself to me as the staff member for the day. He told everybody to introduce themselves to me, so they did. I nodded or grunted in response to each in turn. I was already suffering.

When they were finished, I introduced myself to them and managed to express my desire to become an ex-junkie like them. *Kieran* explained to everybody that I hadn't been to the detox unit and that I was going to be doing cold turkey. He urged everybody to lend their support, especially at night, during the first couple of weeks. Everybody nodded; they'd all been there too. He then said, 'Coolmine Philosophy One,' and handed me a printed card.

'We are here because there is no refuge finally from ourselves. Until a person confronts himself through the minds and hearts of others, he is running.'

They were all rabbitting it off like it was the rosary or something. I continued, self-consciously, to read my printed card.

'Afraid to be alone, he cannot know himself nor any other.'

They reeled off two philosophies inside two minutes and we all sat down again.

When that was over, the Morning Meeting proceeded. *Breda*, my main inquisitor at the interview, continued. She was from the Southwest and quite nice looking, with long dark hair and big brown eyes. She was wearing a hippie-like 'I don't need to dress up' plain floral dress, but the under-emphasis seemed to enhance her beauty. She was holding a clipboard, and she spoke with an air of authority which belied how she looked. That put a quick end to my fantasies, reminding me of the attitude I'd developed to authoritative women. It probably came from having two older sisters and my ma to contend with. She announced the list of people who had court appearances or hospital appointments that day, and informed them that they should be ready to leave immediately after the morning meeting.

With that, *Breda* sat down and said, 'Okay, image blowers.'

Everybody was shouting something but the consensus was that *Henry* should apparently do the 'Funky Chicken'. I didn't know what the fuck was going on, and when *Henry* started doing his impression of a funky chicken while all the assembled sang the tune, I was astounded. It was as mad as anything I'd ever seen back when I was tripping on LSD.

I hadn't a clue how this was supposed to be related to me getting off heroin, but I figured that some of the faces I recognised from the streets must have been there for a while, so obviously something about the methods were working. Still, I couldn't help but feel like I had walked into a lunatic asylum by mistake.

They're all mad, I was thinking to myself, as someone else continued with 'The Funky Gibbon'. Then came Adam Ant and 'Ant Music'. This session ended with an announcement from *Kieran*, the staff member, that we should never forget that 'Image is a killer and fear is your friend.'

I hadn't got a clue what it meant but it seemed important to everybody else, so I nodded agreement. With that, the meeting ended, and everybody went to their work stations. I was told that I was to be crew of the maintenance department and that *Larry* was my department head.

The maintenance department HQ was a little cupboard under the stairs with all the necessary equipment; sweeping brushes, dustpans, buffers, hammers, nails, screws, and the like. I found out that the department consisted of myself and *Larry*. He explained that the assistant department head had split a few days before I arrived.

His first direction was to tell me to sweep the foyer and the hall leading to the kitchen. I didn't set about the task with any great gusto as I was really feeling like shit at this stage, but I obeyed him anyway and set about doing what I was told. I still didn't know what the fuck was going on, or what to make of this place, so I was observing everything going on around me as I swept the floor. Everybody was working away, but in a manner I'd never really seen before. I started sweeping the hall before the kitchen, and listening to the commands being given.

'Hurry up and get those breakfast dishes clean. The expeditor's inspection will be at 10am. Get the pastry ready for lunch. There's pizza on the menu for today.'

I moved back towards the reception area where everybody who had an appointment in town was gathering. I was sweeping, but the floor was spotless to begin with. I'd never seen a cleaner floor. I had cramps in my stomach and goose pimples all over me and I felt like asking if I could go into town with the rest of them, so that I could do a disappearance act, and find some gear, for just one more turn-on. Every limb was aching and filled with agonising pains, my stomach felt like it was tied in a knot, and was being squeezed and twisted like a wet rag, and I could hardly stand up straight. My eyes felt like they were going to fall out of my head at any moment. Jesus, even my hair hurt.

I struggled to hold back the urge to drop the brush and go. Every fibre of my body was screaming at me to get out of there. I wished I could go into detox. Cold turkey was too much for me. Even one week in the detox would make all this madness a little easier to take. I was standing there, lost in thought, staring down the hall towards the exit, when I was interrupted by *Larry*, my boss.

'Are you finished sweeping?'

'Yeah,' I replied.

'Come with me while I check your work.'

I accompanied him back down the hall. He bent down and ran his fingers over the floor and in the nooks and crannies of the doorways.

'This is not acceptable. Sweep it all again.'

I couldn't believe my ears, and I shot him a dirty look.

'Don't react. That's a direction,' he said.

The little culchie bollix, I was thinking to myself. *Who did he think he was talking to?* I could understand if he was a screw in Mountjoy, but he was a 20 year old kid from the South. He didn't even look to me like he'd ever smoked a joint, let alone been a junkie. I was about to say something to him, but changed my mind and just got on with the sweeping.

Ten minutes later, *Larry* came up to me and said, 'Come into the Group Room for a rap.'

We sat down on one of the sofas and he lit up a smoke. I was gumming, and asked him if I could have one too, as he hadn't offered. He said he couldn't, as that was one of the rules of the house—residents couldn't give cigarettes to other residents if they asked for one.

'Everybody gets a ration of 200 a week and no more,' he said. I'd be getting mine as soon as the bus had left for town.

Sure enough, while we were talking, *Willie*, who was the 'crew' of the administration department, came in and gave me 20 Major, and said he'd give me the balance of my ration later on. I ripped open the pack and lit one up.

Larry went on to explain what he had meant about reaction. He explained that all directions must be followed even if I disagreed; after all, I had agreed at the interview to follow all directions. He explained that the dirty look I gave him was a reaction to the direction he had given me to sweep the floor a second time. He said if I felt like that again, I should write my beef down on a piece of paper and put in the slip box in administration. Later I'd be able to bring it up in a group as all groups were 'Hats Off', and everybody in the group had equal status, including the staff. You could pick any bone you liked.

I was almost dizzy from the smoke I'd greedily sucked down as he spoke, as I hadn't had one since I'd arrived the day before. I was nodding agreement with everything he said, though I really hadn't a clue what he was talking about.

He told me, as crew of maintenance and the last one in, I was lowest on the totem pole and had to take directions from everybody. He explained that promotion came from hard work, and with promotion I would also be expected to give those under me directions.

I had no intention of giving anyone directions but I didn't say that to him for fear it might be breaking some other stupid rule. He said it was possible for me to direct someone if I saw them doing something wrong, by using a pull up.

'Pull your brother up before he pulls you down,' was one of the concepts, he explained. 'If you notice someone behaving badly—not getting out of bed on time, or not emptying an ashtray, you pull them up by saying, "I'd like to make you aware you should be out of bed," or, "You haven't emptied your ashtray." They must respond to a pull up the same as to a direction.'

It all sounded so unreal. *I'd like to make you aware*, or, *That's a direction, don't react*. I wasn't one for telling people what to do, and I avoided conflict at all costs, no matter how I felt myself, and with few exceptions, either straight or strung out.

I was willing to listen to him though, as I'd no intention of rocking the boat. I was enjoying sitting there in this nice sunny room having a smoke, as it was keeping my mind off how I felt, and it was better than buffing the floor.

With that, the bell rang and someone shouted, 'Tea break on the lawn.'

Very nice, I thought. It sounded so civilised. *Larry* said I should grab my tea and biscuits and report back to work in 15 minutes. There were a few large teapots set on trays on the lawn beside the driveway and a few packets of Marietta biscuits. I poured myself a cup of tea and was just about to sit down and try and sort out all the thoughts running through my head, when *Victor* came up to me and said, 'Can I rap with you?'

'Sure,' I replied, thinking to myself—*rap; I thought that lingo died with the hippies.*

I knew him from outside. He was one of those posh kids from north county Dublin who had managed to crawl his way over a series of obstacles and into the gutter. He used to have a market stall selling music, which doubled as a groovy hang out for all the cool people during the day.

I'd often seen him in the flats, scoring from the new breed of pushers that had sprung up. I hadn't seen him for a while though, and now I knew why.

'How are you feeling?' he asked.

I felt I could be honest with him as I knew him quite well.

'I feel like fucking shit; I've got cr...'

I didn't get to finish my sentence.

'I'd like to make you aware you shouldn't use bad language on the floor. If you have any feelings you need to deal with, drop a slip. That's a rule of the house.'

'What do you mean on the floor; we're on the lawn.'

'The floor means anywhere outside a group,' he explained. 'I know you feel bad and you're doing cold turkey. We all felt the same when we came in, as we'd only had a week in the detox, so we understand how you feel and we're all willing to help. Any time you need a rap, just let someone know and they'll oblige, day or night. Don't be afraid to ask, especially if you feel like splitting.'

'OK, thanks for the advice,' I replied, thinking to myself, *another rule, another robot.*

He'd only been there a relatively short while, but already he seemed so different, as he explained that he was now the department head of administration, and was responsible for all the paperwork: invoices, receipts, letters liaising with all the residents regarding court cases, hospital visits, social welfare cheques, and so on.

The bell rang to end the tea break. I hadn't managed to tell him how I felt. How do you do that without swearing? I was feeling like shit and all these cunts could do was tell me all the rules and regulations. There were pull ups flying around all over the place as I put my cup back on the tray.

'I'd like to make you aware that you didn't put the cover back on the sugar bowl.'

'I'd like to make you aware you left a full ashtray out on the grass.'

The ones who'd been pulled up just went back and righted their wrong and went about their business.

***

Later, as I was buffing the foyer, I noticed a few people dropping slips in the slip box, mostly the ones who'd been pulled up at tea break. I wanted to get the fuck out of there: pull ups, directions, slips, groups, image blowers. It was mind boggling, and all this on my first day.

I buffed the hall and the foyer and buffed it again after *Larry* inspected it and found it wasn't shiny enough. He had sounded really sympathetic while chatting to me in the Group Room but now he was really acting the bollix. I didn't bother reacting in any way and just got on with it, as it was keeping my mind off how I felt. I made it through until lunch, resisting my urges to leave.

In my heart of hearts, regardless of what I was telling myself about escaping a long sentence, I wanted to get off the gear, get back to where I was when I had given it up the last time. I'd been doing so well until I'd met *Terry* again. I was thinking about this as I grabbed my dinner in the kitchen and made my way into the dining room. I was half-heartedly nibbling away on a pizza, my appetite at zero, when this girl beside me said, 'Eat it up; it will build your strength and you'll need to be strong over the next few weeks. I'm *Una* and I'm the assistant department head of the kitchen. If you don't like the dinner, drop a slip and you can tell us how you feel about it in a group. I've been here eight weeks and the first few weeks were hell but I'm glad now it's over me.'

'The pizza's fine,' I said. 'I just don't feel hungry.'

People were finishing up and bringing their dishes out to the kitchen.

'We can have a rap in the Group Room when lunch is over if you like.'

I felt like it was a direction so I said OK. I really didn't feel like talking to anyone but if I had to, I thought to myself, why not a bird. She was nice looking, about five feet nine, with dark shoulder length hair and a nice refined accent. There were only a couple of people in the Group Room as most of them had gone outside on the lawn after dinner. We sat down in chairs beside the open French windows and it felt like a scene from a movie or something. It was a beautiful day outside.

'How has your first day been so far?' she asked.

I hadn't managed to answer a similar question so far without getting a lecture of some sort so I phrased my answer in a way which I hoped would avoid any more.

'It's been difficult but I realise everybody has been through the same and is willing to help.'

'Yes,' she said, 'that's the nice thing about the Lodge. Everybody here has been through the same thing you're going through now. For me that was the most important part. I've tried to come off dope loads of time in the past, in clinics and psychiatric units here and in London, without any success, but I really think it will work here. I'm determined that it will.'

In keeping with the positive tone and glad to have avoided a pull up, I agreed that I was equally determined, and as the bell sounded to signal the end of lunch hour and back to work she said what I had come to expect.

'If you need to rap about anything, let me know, I'll be glad to help.'

'Thanks,' I said, and made my way to the HQ of the maintenance department—the closet under the stairs—to await my next directions from *Larry*. I was glad I'd managed to have a conversation with somebody without hearing another load of rules and regulations, and though it hadn't been the most interesting of conversations, and certainly not the conversation I would like to have had with a nice looking bird like *Una*, I felt like I had achieved something by not getting hassled or lectured.

Una had seemed nice but this was the same bird I'd heard earlier in the morning shouting out the directions to the poor fucker who was crew of the kitchen, so I'd have to reserve my judgement about her.

***

My first task of the afternoon was to clean the windows, which was quite a daunting task as there were loads of them. *Larry* handed me a load of old newspapers and some window cleaner.

As I was cleaning the windows I was thinking that this place and the people in it reminded me of something; it was a sort of déjà vu, and I was racking my brains when it came to me. It reminded me of when loads of the junkies in town got into Guru Maharaji. They all went to London to listen to his speeches. People were swarming to this little fat 12-year-old Indian kid like he was the Messiah.

After attending enough of his appearances, they were given 'the Knowledge' and a personal mantra which they could repeat over and over again until they 'saw the light'. They all arrived back from these meetings totally changed. They all stopped using dope and set about establishing *ashrams* all over the country. All you could hear out of them was 'the Knowledge' and 'the light' and giving *satsang*. Me and *Aidan* had never given in to the temptation to join the guru and his mob of devotees. We had seen what happened to our mate *Art* when he'd joined the Hare Krishnas, and did a 40 day diet of brown rice.

He had arrived back from London with his long hair shorn, and totally loopy. Me and *Aidan* were back working at the time, having one of our little respites from the gear, and trying to go straight. One evening after work, his ma had said someone had called to the house that day. She gave some strange name but she thought it was *Art*. We called down to his house, hoping it was him, as we hadn't seen him since he'd spent his holidays with us more than a year before. It was in the squat we were living in on Earls Court Road; checking out the hippie lifestyle.

He opened the door. He looked really strange: pale, skinny and bald. His hair had been coming along nicely the year before. He didn't even say hello or invite us in, just walked back into the house and said, 'Would you like a melon to bring home with you?'

Over a year, and this was his first question. The subsequent conversation didn't get any better, although he managed to explain that he'd left his job right after the holiday with us, and returned to London hoping to meet up with us again. But when he got to the squat, it was boarded up and no one was living there anymore. He'd hung around for a couple of weeks until he ran out of bread, and then he had joined the Hare Krishnas. He had just finished his 40 day diet of brown rice. We left *Art*, glad we hadn't fallen into the clutches of the Hare Krishnas 'cos he'd really changed, for the worse as far as we were concerned.

The ones who got into the Guru were much the same. 'The Knowledge' seemed to have a radical effect on people; even *Eamonn*, who had been one of the guys who had first laid the draw on us many years earlier and was a pretty big hash dealer, got into it. He was from the inner-city and could handle himself, by all reports, before he'd gotten into the draw and the hippie thing.

He'd taken a flat in Dublin and turned it into an *ashram*, and he invited me and *Aidan* up one night for some *satsang*, a kind of preaching. He asked us to take off our shoes at the door and we went inside. There were joss sticks lighting everywhere and an altar to the little fat kid.

We thought it was bizarre, and they weren't even smoking any more. Everybody who got 'the Knowledge' became kind of blank, including *Jamie*, who was now a graduate resident here. He and *Jason* and *Johnny*, all the guys from the same area, went to Galway and opened an *ashram*.

They were all the same. They'd all given up the gear and became devotees. It was like they were all hypnotised. Maybe *Jamie* was using some of these methods now in the Lodge, 'cos that's how everyone seemed to me—hypnotised or brainwashed. I was determined I wasn't going to let that happen to me, despite what I'd said to *Una*. I just kept telling myself that I wanted to stay clean and get treated leniently with my court cases, and that was it.

***

I don't know how I felt in the first few days or weeks, except to say that apart from going through horrible withdrawals, I felt safe somehow. Once I got into the rhythm of things and I knew the score, I had a feeling that no one was going to shoot me in the head or slit my throat or anything, which was more than I could say for my life outside. I was obeying every order and taking any pull ups I was given. I was determined to get through this as easily as possible, without upsetting anyone too much in the process. I'd even passed on a bit of feedback. The expeditors came around a few times during the day with their clipboards, collecting the feedback, writing down whatever they were told.

Everybody seemed to have some titbit of info to pass on. I'd listen in any time I could to see what other people were saying, so I could pass on the same bit of information and not feel I was grassing on anyone. It had been explained to me over and over again that the feedback was for the good of the residents. It was just to highlight any changes in someone's behaviour that would indicate they might be getting ready to split. It sounded so nice; you only passed on feedback out of concern for your fellow resident. You weren't ratting on people. To me it seemed so Orwellian. Why didn't they just put video cameras all over the shop so they could watch everything we were doing? After the expeditors collected all the feedback, they'd pass the info on to the Coordinator.

The Coordinator was the resident with the responsibility to coordinate between the residents and the staff. It was the top job in the house. If negotiated successfully, it usually meant that they were at the end of the first phase of getting clean, and would soon be entering phase two, where there was a lot more freedom.

The Coordinator when I started was *Henry*. He was the son of a well respected and wealthy businessman, but had gotten himself strung out. His parents were paying large amounts of money for his treatment in Coolmine. This didn't mean he was treated any differently to the rest of the residents, though. I'd witnessed that at my first morning meeting, when he had treated us to his impersonation of a funky chicken.

After the Coordinator discussed the feedback with the staff, he would go to his office and give directions to bring the people who had been misbehaving to see him. I had noticed this on the afternoon of my first day. I was cleaning the windows in the administration area, which was right beside the Coordinator's office. *Breda* just walked up to this guy *Willie*, who had given me the smokes earlier and who was typing away, and said, 'Stand on the mat outside the Coordinator's office.'

He just stopped what he was doing and stood to attention outside the door. *Breda* went on her way and must have said the same to a few more as there were about six people lined up now, all standing to attention and looking straight ahead, saying nothing.

I was fascinated, and tried to spend as long as I could on this job to see what would happen. There were no mats outside, and I was wondering what the expression meant. Then I heard *Willie* being called in after *Breda* had re-entered the office.

Next I heard *Henry* shouting at the top of his voice, 'You are on the mat because of the sloppy nature of your work and for reacting to a direction from your department head.'

Then *Breda*'s voice chimed in. 'You know *Willie*, that this is junkie behaviour and not up to the standards of this house. This type of behaviour is what got you here in the first place and the outcome for you is a 24 hour bum squad. Report to the department head of maintenance.'

I was wondering what a 'bum squad' was as *Willie* came out of the office and wrote something into a book on the hallstand. He walked straight over to our HQ and reported to *Larry*, who was fixing something under the stairs. I heard *Larry* tell him to help me clean the windows. He then explained to me that for 24 hours, *Willie* was on a bum squad, and as such, was at a lower status than me for the period. He also explained that I wasn't to speak to him at all while he was working in our department. He had to maintain silence and reflect on his bad behaviour and his temporary loss of status. This was also one of the concepts: *Real status, vested status.*

I didn't fancy the idea of standing on the mat at any time in the near future. I doubt if my reaction to being bawled at and given a bum squad would have been as placid as *Willie*'s or any of the others who had been filing in, getting roared at, and filing out again like lambs. None of them seemed to be too bothered by any of it, which made me wonder again about the brain washing.

I witnessed scenes like this every day during the first couple of weeks. It was all so alien and weird, but it seemed to make the time go by quicker. I forgot most of the time how bad I was feeling, until bedtime. To say I suffered would be an understatement. Only someone who has gone through heroin withdrawal can understand the sheer agony of it. It is like every cell in your body is throbbing, and you can do nothing to ease the pain. At the same time your stomach is in bits and you lose control of your bowels. You get so weak that you don't have the energy to get up, or move, or do anything that might take your mind off the pain.

Everybody made good on their promise, however, and I could wake up any of the senior residents and rap to them when I needed to, which was every night for the first couple of weeks. It was weird though. Even in the middle of the night with no one else around there was no way around the 'therapy' talk.

**

I wasn't going to give in to their cure, either; the same kind of cure as always. 'We love you man.'

They were like the 'Jesus freaks'; fucked up in the head, as far as I was concerned. A shower of junkies who were going to show me the way forward? They had got to be fucking joking.

On my second day they brought me into a group. Everyone was silent until another guy, *Henry* came in and said, 'Group on.'

I was pretty amazed at what happened next. There were about 12 people in the group, and they all started picking on this one guy, giving him a horrible time. It was different than when we were working. Here, nobody was following directions.

'Hats Off', they called it; no labels. It was that concept I'd heard earlier, at work now in all its glory: Real Status, vested status. Whatever status you had outside of this group was gone as soon as you sat down. I was amazed when it started 'cos the first thing was a verbal attack by *Breda*, who was the expeditor collecting all the feedback.

She started out on one of the guys from the kitchen. 'What the fuck are you up to? You're reacting all over the floor. Every time anybody gives you a direction, you're glaring at them in a threatening way or asking straight away to go to the slip box—a reaction in itself. You're in here to learn how to control your feelings, not leak them all over the place 'cos you haven't got the balls to be direct and say what you want to say to someone in a group. Behind that hard man image is a scared little boy if you ask me. When are you ever going to learn? You've been on the mat every day for the past week, and as far as I can see you're just setting yourself up to go.'

Jesus Christ!

Her little tirade had been loud, but not emotional.

Next on the kitchen crew's case was *Kevin*, a young guy of about 20. He was crew in the acquisitions department.

'Yes, I agree with *Breda*. We arrived at the same time six weeks ago and you were really doing great. Now, you're breaking every rule in the house. You're a fucking eejit if you think we're impressed. I don't give a bollix what you did outside, yet every chance you get, you're trying to neggy rap (another piece of Coolmine lingo meaning street talk) with me. I came in here to get straight, not to listen to you going on and on about the strokes you pulled. For fuck sake, you're only 20 and you talk as if you're Jesse fucking James. Get a grip or you'll be leaving, and who gives a fuck about you out there—nobody.'

This was getting harsh.

Everybody had a go at him over something, except me. I just sat there mesmerised. When they'd all finished, there was a silence for a while. Then he had his say.

You could tell he was waiting for this. He turned to address *Breda*:

'You, you fucking bitch! You made me make my bed three times yesterday, taking me out of the kitchen when I was really busy, and the bed was OK to begin with. I fucking hate you, you stupid cow.'

He was a young kid from a bad area whose only job up to now had been taking from tills in supermarkets, or anywhere else there happened to be a few quid and a counter in his way. That was the past, however. Now he was the crew of the kitchen in a rehab centre, and he sure had a bone to pick with the expeditor.

As soon as he finished with *Breda*, he had a go at the department head of the kitchen.

'You, you fucking stupid bollix! You made me clean the oven four times on Wednesday. You did it on purpose, you stupid cunt, 'cos you knew the psychiatrists from Grangegorman were coming and we'd be really busy with ten extra dinners. Do you think they were going to inspect the ovens to see if I was alright in the head, you prick?'

That wasn't all. He went around everybody, spitting out all his venom.

I was totally shocked, as I had sort of envisioned us all holding hands and communicating. This wasn't like an *ashram*. This wasn't love and peace. This was a battlefield.

He continued venting his rage and anger.

'You, *Henry* you think you're so fucking perfect, you bastard; strutting around the place with your clipboard. You're like Adolf fucking Hitler and Eva Braun, you and *Breda*, getting your jollies off doling out contracts and bum squads. Concern, my arse! You don't give a fuck about me or anyone else; you and your poxy millions. You know quite well that you're not going to have to worry about money when you get out of here.'

He had a go at everybody, including me, which was a surprise.

'You, you cunt, how the fuck did you get in here without going through the detox? You were stoned when you arrived. I fucking hate you.'

All of a sudden he stopped screaming and started to sob; his elbows on his knees, one hand holding his head, the other wiping the tears from his eyes. The room was totally quiet now except for the sound of his crying. There was a weird kind of sound, coming from deep inside him. It was a scream emerging, but it was coming from the depths of his soul. He wasn't saying anything now, just shaking and moaning. It was like the feeling I'd had when I'd listened to John Lennon's first solo album way back when.

I felt a shiver down my back. The atmosphere was electric. *Breda*, in a completely different tone now, sympathetic and coaxing, said, 'Come on. Let it all out. Let it go. Just dump all that shit you've been carrying around.'

Henry, the staff member in charge of the group, made similar exhortations. It seemed to work. The sobbing stopped but the moan continued and got louder. His head was now down between his legs, his arms dangling by his sides, and he was screaming, screaming with all his heart and soul.

'I hate you. I hate you, you stupid fucking imagey cunt. You useless motherfucker.'

He went on and on screaming out his hate at the floor. When he was finished, one of the guys asked him 'Who do you hate?'

'Myself,' he replied, still staring at the floor. With that, he broke down in tears, deep, touching tears, and when it seemed like they'd never stop, everyone in the group got up and moved towards him, and sat down around him, and touched him, and empathised with him, and finally, everyone gave him a hug.

'Everything will be alright. It's good that you got rid of all that shit.'

I even went over to him myself. Even though I didn't know him, I felt like I did. I felt sorry for him.

After he regained his composure, he sat back upright. He'd stopped crying now and his face had a glow. Someone asked him if there was anything he wanted to talk about and he said there was. He went on to tell us about his life; no crying or screaming, just matter of fact.

He'd been adopted but didn't find out 'til his teens. He told us how he felt about this, how he suddenly felt like an outsider in his own family. He talked about his adoptive parents, his brothers and sisters. When he was finished, the group ended with everybody giving him another hug. I didn't know him from Adam but I'd witnessed something that I'd never seen before. The atmosphere of love and real concern didn't go away, and he looked totally different—

he glowed. He seemed lighter and softer, in some way transformed.

Hugs are medicine: another concept. But this one seemed to sink in.

He didn't split.

That very fact made me think that maybe there was something to all of this. It all seemed strange, and at times downright weird, but I couldn't argue with the results, so I vowed to stick it out.

***

After about three months I was well into the swing of things. I had gone from crew of maintenance to crew of administration and then assistant department head of administration. I had earned myself some privileges— sending and receiving letters, and eventually phone calls. I had written to my family, and also to *Sarah*, who to my total surprise, actually replied. I had never known her to write to anybody before, and although I had written her a very honest letter I was surprised that she had written back. I hadn't really had any contact with her since I had gone back on the gear, almost two years earlier.

I was in love with her again, or should I say, still. It had been easy when I was stoned to forget about her or just forget my feelings for her. Especially when I had someone like *Jodie* mothering me and making sure I had everything I needed, which was really only one thing—drug money.

Even when I'd bumped into her in the pubs we used to frequent, or one of the clubs in town, she'd totally ignore me as if I didn't, and had never, existed.

But this reply gave me more of a reason to keep the thought going that maybe the two of us might have a future together, after all that had happened. When I was finally allowed telephone calls, she was the only one I talked to once a week. I'd tell her about the progress I was making; how the therapy worked, the groups, and so on. Then one week I called her as usual, and she dropped it on me. She had given up her job and was emigrating to Spain. I was devastated but wished her all the best. She had never lived outside of Ireland before and wanted to give it a try.

I tried to keep on going and put it out of my head but I was getting fed up with Coolmine. I didn't want to listen to other residents' problems and feed them full of concepts and philosophies. I'd been there three months, and I was in the period they referred to as the therapy hum; the danger period when many people split, and as predicted, I was feeling the same way myself.

I had been in many groups now, at least two a week since I'd been there. But no one ever really confronted me about anything, except once when I'd finally finished my cold turkey and was sleeping normally. I was confronted for singing and generally being happy all the time. One of them confronted me and said I was acting as if I was in a holiday camp. I replied that that was one of the concepts: *Act as if, think as if, feel as if, and be.*

The discussion got a little heated but I didn't break down and cry or scream or do any of the other shit I'd seen other people doing. I was holding my own on the floor and living by the rules. I wasn't often on the mat for bad behaviour, just niggly stuff like not getting up on time. But now I was sick of it all, especially since *Sarah* had told me she was leaving. I had been promoted to department head of maintenance, and the next steps after that were expeditor, Coordinator and then re-entry phase two; then freedom.

***

My initial reason for being there turned out to be a good move. I had gotten off lightly in court. Instead of what would have been a certain long stretch, I had gotten a long remand to see what my progress would be in treatment. So in that sense, things were looking good. But no matter what way I thought it through, I couldn't see myself staying much longer. I could see that people were getting results, and I was obviously staying off the gear, but the therapy speak was driving me nuts.

I began to slack off a bit. I found I couldn't give directions with any degree of commitment. I couldn't be bothered pulling anybody up. I didn't want to rap with anyone. All this change in my behaviour was passed on as feedback and I suddenly found myself on the mat outside the Coordinators office more and more often.

I even got my first bum squad in the kitchen, cleaning the ovens. I was glad of the 24 hour respite, taking orders and not giving them, and best of all not having to speak to anyone for a whole day. It was a welcome break from the drudgery it had all become to just say nothing, and do my bit.

The next outcome after being on the mat was worse though. I was demoted back down to crew of kitchen, and lost all my privileges. I didn't really mind the demotion as I thought the whole system was idiotic anyway, but losing my privileges really pissed me off. I wouldn't be able to talk to *Sarah* again before she left, or even be able to send her a letter. It would take weeks before I earned those privileges back, and in the meantime, she would be gone. There were a lot of things going on in my mind, things I had to discuss with her before she left, and the idea of leaving wouldn't go away.

On a Tuesday night I went into the group as usual. As soon as it started I was attacked from all sides.

'You, you stupid prick, what the fuck are you up to? You were doing great and now you're acting out all over the place, like a big child. When are you going to grow up?'

I got it from all sides, from all the senior residents who were in this group. They must have dropped a lot of slips on me because they went on and on. After about 15 minutes, when they had all said their piece, it was my turn. I didn't roar or scream or anything. I kept my composure. I could have said a lot about each and every one of them. I had bones to pick with them all but I'd been in enough groups to know that all they wanted was for me to start shouting and roaring at them and then finally break down. I wasn't going to go for it and I just regaled them with a very clinical and rational explanation for my recent behaviour.

I was going to tell them how I felt about *Sarah* emigrating to Spain, and how maybe I'd never see her again, but I didn't. When nothing else was forthcoming from me, everybody accepted it and the group moved on to some other poor unfortunate who needed their concern. I just bided my time until it was over.

The next day I got stuck into my job as crew of kitchen. It was hectic but I liked it as it was the only real job in the house. It had real schedules and real results. People needed to be fed, three or four times a day. I was thinking all the time about how I was going to split. It was recommended that when you were thinking like this, you should sit on the bench again and think things over. But I was in no mood for a second review of my life.

I had seen this happen a few times. Someone just sat on the bench when things got too much. It usually ended with a special group, and the person remained, after a good scream or a rap or whatever was necessary. Some people split, even after sitting on the bench for a think. Others just upped and left, sometimes never to come back again, or maybe many years later, a little more haggard and worn out, and a little more desperate.

I thought about all my options and why I was thinking of taking this step. I was up to my neck in the therapy. I thought the groups were a load of crap. They might work for other people, but not for me, not anymore, and I wanted to see *Sarah* before she left for Spain. At 10pm that night, I walked out the door and down the driveway, without looking back once, and got the bus from Clonsilla into town. I didn't have any bus fare but that was the least of my worries. I'd escaped.

Even though there were no cells, bars, walls or guards, I felt like I'd escaped.

I arrived in town about 10.30pm and I was impressed by its ordinariness. It made me feel like one of the crowd, and I realised that's exactly how I wanted to be—ordinary; no-one prying into my soul or examining every aspect of my behaviour. No one-on-one raps, or group hugs to make me feel loved and cared for. I wanted to be surrounded by people who couldn't care less, people who just wanted to get home and go to bed.

I had no problem about the bus fare from the bus conductor on the Clonsilla bus. I just gave him my name and address. It was comforting to know things remained the same outside. I jumped on another bus on Fleet Street and headed for my ma's.

She had attended a couple of parents' meetings sponsored by Coolmine, and I knew she had been advised about the tough love policy; not to allow your son or daughter to come home after they had split. But I was confident that wouldn't be a problem. I don't think she really believed I was a junkie in the first place, despite everything. The bus conductor on this bus was equally as understanding as the conductor on the other bus, and I arrived home at about 11.10pm. All the lights were off, so I had to knock on the door. It was opened by my younger brother Johnny.

'What are you doing here?' he asked me sleepily.

'I left Coolmine,' I replied.

'Come on in and go to bed.'

That's exactly what I did. I went straight to bed and fell fast asleep. I had gotten used to the routine in the Lodge; work hard and sleep hard. When I woke up the next morning, my brothers Johnny and Peter had already left for work. I went downstairs and my ma was in the kitchen, listening to the *Gay Byrne Show* on the radio. She wasn't surprised to see me. Johnny had told her I was home. She asked me why I had left and I told her the truth. I told her I wanted to see *Sarah* before she left for Spain, and that maybe I'd go back in when I had done so.

She accepted that and made me breakfast and we chatted away for a couple of hours. After lunch I asked her for a loan of a few quid. She obliged, and I headed into town to meet *Sarah*. I spent Friday and Saturday with her, and said my goodbyes. I explained my behaviour as best I could—my descent into being a fully-fledged addict again.

I apologised for having hurt and embarrassed her when we were together, and wished her all the best for the future, asking her to keep in touch.

I was hoping she might ask me to go with her, or say she loved me and couldn't live without me. She told me it would be a long time again before she could trust me, but that going through therapy was a step in the right direction. All was not lost.

CHAPTER 13

I called the Lodge on the Monday morning and asked if I could come back, and they said yes. I made my way out there and sat on the bench again.

I wasn't long on the bench this time, and I didn't do a lot of thinking. I knew what was coming—a general meeting, followed by a shaved head and a dishpan or a work contract.

The general meetings were attended by everyone in the community, staff and residents alike. A bell was rung as a signal for everyone to come to the Group Room for a meeting. I heard everyone trooping past as I sat there facing the wall. After a few minutes, I was called in and told to stand with my back to the wall. The whole community would then decide if I could return or not.

It was the same as a Hats Off meeting and everybody let me know how they felt about me splitting. I was told in no uncertain terms that it would be a long time before they would trust me again. I was asked if I'd gotten stoned and I replied honestly, with some pride, that I hadn't. I had to give a commitment of some sort to show that I was serious now about getting clean. I agreed to a shaved head and a dishpan contract. I was also to wear a sign, 'This is my Image' as they told me I'd never really revealed my true self in a group.

I was taken upstairs to the bathroom to have my head shaved. It was a weird feeling, as I'd never been bald before. It was done in complete silence as it was up to me, 'the contract', to initiate conversation with the opener, by saying, 'Can I rap to you please?' but I was in no humour for conversation as my shorn locks fell to the floor.

Being the dish pan contract meant that I received all directions from the department head of the kitchen, and no one else could communicate with me. I could communicate with them at mealtimes if I wished, by formally asking for a rap. The department head would wake me up in the morning, a half an hour earlier than everybody else, to buff out the kitchen and prepare the tables for breakfast.

After breakfast, it was into the dishpan to wash all the dishes, pots and pans. When I was finished, the department head would inspect my work, and then tell me to do it all again.

The first couple of days in the dishpan were strange. I had now become the lowest of the low, as it were, and that was exactly how it felt. This whole journey of escapism had started out with a desire to let my hair grow, so to speak, as a way to show my desire for love and peace. Now here I was, locks shorn, lower than a skinhead, hairless, broken and wondering why I'd subjected myself to this, wondering why there was nowhere else to go.

There was a specific set of rules with regard to 'the contract', as I was referred to on the administration board. I was somewhere below crew, and seemed to get lower every day. I looked at the board on my way to lunch. Maybe whoever was crew of admin was trying to tell me I was sinking. It was lost on me because I didn't think it was possible to get any lower. I felt really small and humiliated.

For the first couple of days, it was nice to wash the dishes in silence. I had just spent the weekend with one of the most beautiful women in the world. I hadn't shot any dope or got drunk or done anything wayward. I had spent hours in *Sarah*'s house, talking and laughing, and having a good time, remembering the good things about the past.

I'd kissed her goodnight at the front door before taking the two mile walk up to my house. I'd been happy to do that before flopping into bed in my ma's place, and falling asleep, drug and alcohol free. Fuck me, I was cured!

I would have loved to have had the means to offer *Sarah* an alternative, a future in the sun together, maybe. But I didn't even have the bus fare into town, or back to Coolmine, for that matter. I had to borrow that from my ma.

I'd managed it anyway, getting the bus fare that is, and here I was, shaven headed and working like a slave in the dishpan. I wondered what *Sarah* would have thought of me now.

These were my thoughts in the first couple of days. The feelings I had when some visitors would come to visit the lodge were unbelievable. Groups of nurses or nuns or priests, or whatever, who were expressing an interest in this fascinating project, and as they stood in front of the dishpan door, having all the procedures explained to them by some resident or another, I felt like shit, trying to force a smile as they explained what the 'contract' was, and the reason for the soggy cardboard sign around my neck stating: 'This is my image.'

I certainly wasn't in the humour for talking; so I used these first few days to avoid asking anybody for a rap. I went silent on the same people I had been proselytising, directing and pulling up, only a few days before. It felt good, like I didn't need them. It sort of proved to them I was better than the average Joe Soap ex-junkie.

After three days in the dishpan, I had something in my head to say about all of them. I asked my 'boss' if I could drop a few slips. I wanted to let them know how it felt, how it was to clean up after them after every meal, particularly as they seemed to take great delight in slopping their leftovers on the outside of the plastic slop bag, knowing there was a 'contract' to clean it all up.

I could see them all from the bottom up, and it wasn't a pleasant sight. I couldn't wait to get in a group with some of these motherfuckers, where status was left outside the door.

The first group I was in after dropping all the slips had no one in it I'd dropped slips on. I couldn't believe it. It was all new residents talking about the same old shit.

'You didn't get out of bed on time; you didn't empty your ashtray.'

This was a deliberate move by the staff to let me sit on my feelings for a while longer. I'd be dropping a few slips on the staff as soon as this group was over. There was absolutely no dynamic in this group, no way of getting off a few 'lings', as feelings were called in Coolmine speak. I finally understood one of the other peculiarities of language they liked to use. The whole fucking community was 'coming out' all over me.

I was livid as I made my way down to the dishpan to prepare supper for them all. When I'd washed up, after they had all finished and were tucked up safely in their beds, I was angry enough to kill. I wouldn't stick much more of this shit. I was getting to bed in the early hours of the morning having waited and scrubbed up after all these ungrateful fuckers, and I'd be getting up again at 5.30am to start all over again. I was exhausted and angry.

I noticed now, at mealtimes, some of my old peers always trying to sit beside me, to see if I would ask them for a rap. They knew I would be itching to talk to someone, to let it all out. I resisted the temptation, but by the end of the first week as the 'contract', I needed to talk to someone. I was ready to split again.

I thought about it all the time as I washed the dishes or cleaned the floor, but I couldn't imagine walking around with a bald head outside of here. I looked like shit. This was definitely not my image. Anyway, there was nowhere to go. No *Sarah*, no *Jodie*, no money. I felt well and truly trapped.

I finally began to talk to some of my peers during meal times and breaks, but without going into any deep shit. More often than not it was about their problems, not mine. It was like where we had left off before I had decided to split.

These little moments of respite gave me the strength to continue. It was even better when one of the residents from the re-entry house came in and talked to me—normal people—like the guy who had first interviewed me a few months before in Jervis Street.

He was feeling great now as he had found a job not far away in a galvanising plant. He told me how he had nearly shit a brick when 'The General' Martin Cahill had come in to the company where he worked to have the chrome on his Harley upgraded. He said he was full of mixed feelings. Firstly, he had just been promoted and felt like he was being watched by everybody, and he thought everyone in the job would know who 'The General' was and wonder about him when he had expressed a surprised delight in seeing this guy there. Given time to reflect on the whole situation, he realised that it was more of a feather in his cap. The boss probably felt better about promoting him, realising now that he was such a good friend of people like that. After all, there weren't many Harley owners in Dublin in 1981.

He would drag me into the dining room to smoke a few fags, telling me to forget about the dishes. He'd regale me with these stories of the outside, and although I had been outside only a few days earlier, it was different talking to him about all the old heads he was bumping into, how he was coping as one of those 'freaks' from Coolmine who didn't get stoned anymore. I really appreciated the 'neggy rap' in the middle of all the therapeutic nonsense.

I never, ever had days like the days I had in the dishpan. By day five, I had stubble on my head. It was one of my only intimate moments, playing with my own hair. It made me realise there was a sense of touch to recover.

My senses had been dulled by drug abuse in the worst possible way; I had started to feel that I wasn't really sensing anything unless I was high. That was all changing now though. I found myself touching my head more often, and I felt like Samson regaining his strength.

***

I had been in there four months now and hadn't had any sex. The very fact that I realised this gave me a sort of satisfaction and made me think about how well I was coming along. I had gotten my sense of touch restored, and now here I was regaining the libido I had left behind when heroin took over.

Sure, I had managed to kiss *Sarah* a couple of times when I was out, but that was just a peck on the cheek. A hug after a group was probably more intimate. It was impossible to have sex in there, and even a wank was out of the question. The only moment of privacy I'd had since I'd arrived was when I was having a shit, and even that wasn't totally private. Someone was sure to follow up with a pull up in the group room after lunch.

'I'd like to make you aware that someone didn't clean the toilet in dormitory one,' or, 'Someone didn't replace the toilet roll in the women's dorm.'

A wank was definitely out of the question. A ride was out of the answer.

But sometimes there were beautiful women in there.

A new girl arrived while I was in the dishpan. I felt like a real prick at her first morning meeting. I had known her on the outside. She was one of the new generation of junkies, and I had often given her a turn-on or sold her a few bags of above average gear. Back then when I was Shay, one of the gang—pretty much a made man.

She was absolutely gorgeous, in a sad-eyed Twiggy-ish, blonde kind of way; massive eyes, framed in a sad skeletal face. She looked like the Blessed Virgin.

I'd never managed to fuck her when I was outside and knew I never would in here, not with my bald head, and sign, and no oversized ten-pound bags of scag to impress her. I felt like shit as I introduced myself to her. 'I'm Shay, the dishpan contract.'

***

I just couldn't get over how hard my first week as the contract was. On the Saturday I got up and prepared the tables for breakfast as usual, and washed up afterwards. There weren't that many people buzzing around. As I scrubbed out some pot which had contained burned scrambled eggs—knowing that I would probably have to do it three times again before the department head was satisfied—I could hear everybody getting ready for their weekly trip to the swimming pool, about a mile down the road. I could hear excited voices, and it reminded me of the sound of the school yard from far away.

It made me feel nostalgic, thinking back to how the school yard in Drimnagh used to sound when I was doing the rounds with Dermot, the vegetable man, for thruppence and an apple and an orange. I used to do that for a quarter of an hour when we got out of school at lunchtime, and a quarter of an hour before going back.

I could hear the sound of the schoolyard, like a mass happiness, and I knew by the pitch what time it was, when it was time to finish with Dermot and head back, just in time for the last water drinking competition, or to see who could smoke the most fags behind the bicycle sheds, just in time for the crescendo, before the bell rang and it was time to head back into our classrooms. That was the way I felt in the dishpan on the first Saturday as they all prepared to go to the baths, and then left me in that awful 'back into the classroom' imposed silence.

There was suddenly no staff in the house, just me and *Phil*, my department head. He was missing his weekly trip to the baths too, but now on day five, he was beginning to become more of a human, and was starting to treat me as something approaching human. He came down to the pan about 15 minutes after they had all left for the baths to check on my work. I was getting quite good at it, making every effort to have every pot, pan, dish and spoon sparkle on the first go, making it more difficult for him to find a mistake and tell me to do it again. He did a quick check, and told me to take a break and have a smoke in the dining room. As I was lighting my first Major of the day, *Phil* made his way over to the Group Room and put on a couple of album tracks—The Moody Blues, Bowie, The Beatles. I was on my fifth Major before the rest of them arrived back from the swimming pool for lunch. *Phil* and I weren't talking, but at least we were communicating.

Without any direction, I got up, emptied my ashtray and set the table for lunch; I didn't need any more direction. I felt somehow close to *Phil* just then. It was like we had finally reached an understanding, a common acceptance that we were both in this together and were battling through, like two veteran soldiers who had seen too much and no longer needed to, or wanted to, talk about it. But I was still struggling with my own thoughts, my unease, and my desire to get out of there.

I asked *Una* for a rap during lunch and told her how I was feeling: small and ready to split all the time. She was feeling much the same herself. She had been to the doctor during the week and he had confirmed she was pregnant. Her boyfriend, the father, was still outside shooting dope, and she wasn't allowed to communicate with him. She was torn between splitting to tell him the good news, in the hope he might see sense and seek treatment, or going with the advice of all the other residents and staff; that her responsibility was to herself and her unborn baby to get clean, and that continuing in the negative contract with her boyfriend could only end in disaster.

We talked about this constant dilemma between staying and leaving. Even though there were no bars on the windows, or walls to keep us in, there was something inside us keeping us there. We had created our own bars and walls through lack of choice. I had split just over a week before, and now I was the lowest of the low—worse off than when I'd started. It definitely felt that way anyway, and I told her so. My advice to her was the same as everybody else's: stay put, and finish it out. It would be no fun out on the mean streets, with an ever growing belly and a continually emptying pocket. And from what I knew of her boyfriend, he wouldn't be too keen on sharing the load.

I got stuck into the afternoon clean-up with a great intensity, almost obsessively, determined that *Phil* would find no mistake in my work. I wanted to have the shiniest, cleanest pots and pans; it kept my mind off other things.

The rest of the weekend went by without any great problems. *Phil* was even finding it difficult to find things for me to do, and had me buffing floors and cleaning windows, over and over again.

It was like I had become invisible. During the first couple of days of the contract, I had the feeling nobody wanted to look at me; not just because of the change in my appearance, and my loss of status, but because I represented the ultimate trap. I had left and voluntarily come back. Now, after a week, no one seemed to notice me at all as I went about my menial tasks, buffing and scrubbing like the proverbial fly on the wall. It was interesting to watch everybody.

They were preparing for a sensitivity group, a non-confrontational peace and love type of thing. The senior residents were directing all the new arrivals to bring all the mattresses down from the bedrooms, and pile them up outside the Group Room. They all had that look of anticipation, having participated in those kinds of groups before. The newer residents looked mesmerised and apprehensive—another piece of madness, to add to all the madness they were already experiencing with the directions, pull ups, feedback and groups; watching people spitting out their 'lings' at the floor, and the hugs and encouraging words afterwards.

They all had one thing in common. They looked like kids, like children in a nursery school preparing a game of musical chairs or blind-man's-buff. No one could guess by looking at them that they were all recovering addicts who had wreaked havoc on society while on the outside. But as they ran around preparing for this sensitivity group, they all looked perfectly innocent.

**

The second week of the contract continued in much the same way, but I was noticing more and more how people were 'coming out' on me—still deliberately missing the bin with their leftovers, leaving me more to clean. They were beginning to annoy me more and more and I could feel myself getting angrier with every passing hour. I would let it build up and ask *Phil* after a couple of hours if I could drop some slips.

I had dropped a lot of slips by the time the drug squad came to play their football game with the residents on the Wednesday. I was in the pan, washing the extra dishes when it started. Tears just kept welling up in my eyes and I couldn't stop them, waves and waves of them. Like when I was back on the bench after I first arrived, a picture book of memories kept coming back to me.

I was back in the hospital, watching my da dying, and it was as real as it had been way back then. All the emotions I had felt back then; the sadness, the anger, the despair, flooded over me. I couldn't wash anymore, so I went looking for *Phil*. Everybody else was at the game. I asked him if I could have a rap and he said, 'Yeah.'

I let it all pour out. It lasted about ten minutes. I had regained my composure and was back working when they all came in after the game, giving me more dishes to wash. After I had washed up once again, it was time for a group.

The group had only started when one of the guys put it on me, by asking how I was getting on. I told everybody what had happened with *Phil* that afternoon, and I started to sob again, long uncontrollable sobs. Someone else coaxed me, and asked me what I'd like to say to my da. I said I'd like to say, 'I love you.'

'Then say it,' he said.

Half-crying still, I said it. Then he asked me what else I'd like to say, and I asked him what he meant. He asked again, 'What else would you like to say to your da?' and in the silence, it started. It went from a sob, to a scream, and still a louder scream until finally it blurted out:

'I hate you, you motherfucker. I hate you, you fucking bollix.'

On and on I went, and with my last bit of energy, I got it out—'Why did you abandon me?'

It had taken a long time to come; the guts of 13 years, most of them under the influence of drugs in a failed attempt to escape from the reality I didn't want to face. But now it was out.

The next day I put in a memo to the staff to get off the contract, explaining what I had learned, and my request was granted.

Doing the dishpan contract taught me what I needed to learn. It made me realise that I was angry, and that my anger at my father's death had led to my antisocial behaviour, which spiralled into full-blown drug addiction and a string of criminal charges that only furthered my descent into the world of drugs.

The realisation was like a weight off my shoulders, an indescribable release of a terrible burden that had hung over me, pushing me down, for over a decade.

My descent into drug addiction had nothing to do with where I was from or how I was brought up, because I had a good childhood, and I could see that there were a lot of quite wealthy people in the Lodge too anyway. It was all about anger, and a desire to escape from the reality I just didn't want to accept; one where people like my da suffered horrendous pain and became an empty shell of his former self.

I saw that taking drugs gave me respite, helped me tackle life's problems, because in the skewed reasoning of a drug addict, life's problems become very different to those you used to have. The only problem an addict faces is how to get more drugs. You don't care about anything or anybody else, at least not when you're stoned, because all that matters right then is you and the drug you are about to ingest.

When, or if you snap out of it, you start to come back to reality, and when that happens, you realise you now have more problems to face than before, so it is easier to just slip back into an altered reality again.

I realised that my drug abuse was a defence mechanism too. In my opinion, heroin is the worst such drug because as soon as you take it, it changes your life forever. Few people who get as seriously into it as I did manage to crawl back out of its clutches, and it was only then, when I realised there was some deeper reason behind what I was doing, that I managed to start turning my life around.

Nobody wants to stick a needle in their arm every day unless something is wrong. Heroin makes you sick, but not just in the obvious ways; it causes you to see things differently, or to put it a better way, not to see things at all. It makes you think that what you are doing is OK—better than OK—absolutely perfect, so you can ask yourself why you would ever want to stop using it.

It's seductive, but it's deadly. It makes you feel so good, fooling you into thinking you've never felt better, while all the time it is slowly killing you. All of this just suddenly washed over me, like the rays of the sun giving light to the dawn.

Jesus. My unrealised emotions had led me to nearly ruin my life. I had lost *Sarah*, had gained a criminal record, and had ravaged my body with drugs. But now I knew the root cause, I could address it and move on. I made rapid progress after that.

***

I finished the first phase of the therapy towards the end of 1982, having completed a successful two months as Coordinator and a couple of weeks without a title so that I could come down from the power trip, and get ready for the re-entry phase.

This second phase was to prepare us for the real world, where there wouldn't always be one of your peers around to pull you up and make you aware where you were going wrong, and where there wouldn't always be groups where you could vent your feelings and frustrations.

It was a much less disciplined and freer environment, totally unlike the highly disciplined and hard-working ethic of phase one. The emphasis here was to put oneself under pressure, to keep the standards learned in the first part, and also to look for a job and find accommodation for a move back to the real world.

There was a trained psychologist on hand during the day to help with any problems that might occur. There was also a group once a week, albeit, a much more low key affair than the groups in the phase one house.

Everybody had their own room; a welcome bit of privacy, having spent more than a year in a dormitory. There was also an allowance of £10 a week. That seemed like a fortune, having only had access to money a couple of times in the previous 18 months. All in all, it was a little bit of freedom, the chance to write a letter, make a phone call, venture outside the grounds without writing a memo to the staff—little things to be appreciated like never before.

I had been a little bit luckier than the rest in so far as I was the only one with a driver's licence. I had been in the outside world more than most in the previous three months, since we'd had a van donated.

I had even managed to meet *Sarah* once, without anybody knowing. She was back now, having spent a year in Spain. I had been collecting paint, which was donated to us by a company in Drimnagh. The company was near her house, and she came around to meet me. She looked really gorgeous, in a yellow tank top and black jeans, and she was deeply tanned. We only spent a few minutes together but she was happy that I had stuck it out in Coolmine and was glad I was nearly finished. She told me a bit about her time in Spain. It had been her first time living away from home. She mentioned a couple of guys she had been going out with over there, but it didn't seem like there was any big love in her life right then. We left each other with a quick peck on the cheek and a promise to keep in touch when I was free to do so. It was a promise I intended to keep.

CHAPTER 14

As soon as I got into re-entry, I started to call *Sarah* quite regularly. Sometimes we'd talk for hours on the phone. It was almost as if all the shit that had gone down was now forgotten, and even forgiven.

She was hanging around again with *Orla*, who lived around the corner from her house in Drimnagh. They had hung out together all the time when I was on the gear, and I used to see them together in all the pubs in town. *Orla* had really been a big influence on her. She was a punk. *Sarah* changed her style completely when they started hanging out. She'd gone from staid suits to bovver boots.

I liked *Orla*, and even though *Sarah* ignored me all the time I was back on the gear, *Orla* never did. In fact, one night, after I stumbled into a pub after getting a kick in the bollix from a guy who'd caught me totally by surprise getting out of a taxi—I owed him a few quid—*Orla* had gone out of her way to buy me a drink and check he was gone.

She'd let me stash some clothes in her house before I went into Coolmine. She'd never told *Sarah*, even though they were hanging out together, because she had become very anti-drugs. Not surprising really, seeing as it had ruined our relationship. But things had changed.

Our relationship during this time didn't go beyond the phone calls and visits to see her in the department store where she'd started to work again. I didn't dare to ask her out, as I wasn't sure what her reaction would be. Anyway, £10 a week, pocket money, didn't buy a lot then. It would barely stretch to a night out at the movies, and during our time together, going to the movies was not one of our favourite pastimes. We normally spent the evenings in one of the groovier pubs in town, drinking as much as possible 'til closing time. This was followed by a visit to one of the many clubs in town, to imbibe large quantities of wine.

Abstaining from alcohol was the main rule of the second phase of the therapy though, in addition to the normal rules of the house. It was felt that even though we were all there to cure our drug addiction, abusing alcohol could lead to drugs. It was even recommended that we should continue our on-going cure by attending Narcotics Anonymous, which is similar to AA.

The major problem for most of the people in re-entry was finding a job. Being a graduate of a therapeutic community like the Lodge was not necessarily a great recommendation to a prospective new employer. By the time I arrived there were 12 people in phase two—all unemployed, and one in phase three. That was the guy who had interviewed me 18 months earlier. Now he had a job and his own apartment—the only one to have fulfilled the criteria for phase three: independence from Coolmine, and drug free.

I was determined to get a job, as soon as possible, and luckily for me, there was always someone looking for a salesman. I found a job selling contracts for slot machines on a commission only basis, but with a company car.

I'd work all day, driving around from amusement arcades to snooker halls to shops, looking for customers who would allow me to set up a machine on their premises. The profits were to be split on a 50/50 basis.

It seemed like an easy pitch. We provided the machines for nothing, and the owner of the premises collected half the take. My commission was 75% of the first eight weeks' take. As these machines were capable of taking large amounts of money, I was looking forward to some good commission cheques.

However, there were some disadvantages. The first one being, gaming machines were, strictly speaking, illegal in Dublin. Although the law was seldom applied to the letter, some potential customers were reluctant to take a chance and endanger their main business. The second disadvantage for me, as an ex-addict, was that anyone who was willing to take the chance was usually a business on the fringes of the law anyway. I found myself spending a lot of time hanging around the inner city in gaming halls, which of course, went hand in hand with illegal drugs. Temptation was all around. It was like a recovering alcoholic getting a job in a brewery. The third disadvantage was that my commission basis was 75% of the first eight weeks' take, and as was often the case, the machine was broken into and robbed well before I got paid.

On the bright side, though, I was out and about every day, and spent a lot of my time just driving around and visiting people I knew, and making it back to the Lodge before midnight. In the weekly groups, I was asked how I was getting on in the job. Although everybody had been happy for me that I got a job so quickly, it was no secret that a lot of people felt that selling gaming machines was not unlike selling drugs. It was, however, a subject that was not heavily pursued. Everybody in re-entry was bending the rules to some degree, and even though we had all been forewarned of the consequences of a negative contract, there was one developing.

I was the latest arrival and didn't notice it at first. In fact, I thought the low key tone of the groups was the way it was supposed to be; less hysterical than the heavy confrontations in the first part. Because I had a job, I wasn't around for much of what went on during the day. Most mornings, I would set off about 9am for the office, and inform the boss of any progress or lack of it I was making. I also gave a lift to anyone who wanted to go into town. They were all grateful for that, as it saved them some money, and left them with an extra couple of bob for smarties or fruit gums.

We were all like big kids really. The Lodge was like the family home. We had our pocket money, and had to be home at 12. The only difference was, we were aged between 23 and 35, and between us, and we had been responsible for grave misdeeds before we went in. And now here we were, after a year and a half; model citizens.

The boredom and the lack of funds made life very difficult and the lack of structure after phase one made it even more so. It was almost as if everyone missed the hierarchical structure and the intense self-examination of the groups. I was away most of the day, but having no one to tell me what to do, I spent most of my time just screwing around; going up to my ma's for breakfast, and staying as long as I could; making a couple of token calls to amusement arcades or snooker halls, to see if they wanted some new machines. But more often than not, I was just playing a couple of games of snooker, or playing the slots myself.

My partner in the re-entry phase was *Jason*. He was the youngest, in his early twenties, and the one who seemed best adjusted to the whole situation. He was from a good area—one of the new breed of junkies from the posher parts of the Southside.

He probably had more problems than most of us. Two of his older brothers were strung out, so going home for him just meant hanging around with junkies. I was working less and less, and *Jason* would spend most of the day with me, driving around just to pass the time. Sometimes we'd go to the movies on free passes, hustled from the management by the acquisitions department in phase one. They were eager to help anyone who was trying to make a go of things. More often than not, we'd go and visit *Sarah* in work afterwards. She didn't mind me bringing *Jason* in, as he looked respectable and was from a nice area. I was always in my working gear—suit and tie—back to my pre-Coolmine old self, with one exception; I had no money.

Jason was the one who kept me informed of all the comings and goings in the Lodge. He had been in re-entry about three months before me, but still didn't have a job. He earned a little bit extra by working as a part time staff member, leading groups and looking after the day to day running of things at the weekends.

I used to make it a point to go over to the phase one house at the weekends, and have a chat with some of the residents there. I knew they liked that, as I'd enjoyed it when I was there. A chance for a normal conversation, without the constraints of the therapy, or a neggy rap. I'd find the ones who couldn't handle their cigarette ration of 200 a week, just like I hadn't been able to when I was there. As a resident, you weren't allowed to ask for a smoke but you could accept as many as you were offered. I used to love it on Sundays when I was gumming for a smoke and someone would come over and give me a few to last me 'til Monday morning.

As *Jason* began to trust me more, he told me about some of the things that were going on, which shouldn't have been. He told me that some people on the programme, who were also in phase two, were hanging around with a gang whom he knew to be still big into dope in the posher areas of the Northside—Howth and Malahide.

I wasn't really surprised. I had noticed on one of the open days, which we'd had when I was still in the first phase, a few visitors, who I remembered from when I was outside as being really into the dope. They weren't junkies, but avowed ganja heads, with their long hair, cool gear and posh accents. They had spent most of their time with one of the members of the group that day. I presumed they had given it up or something, and wanted to talk to him about it.

It wasn't as if everyone who smoked a bit of dope was to be avoided totally. It would have been practically impossible. But it was certainly impressed upon everybody not to drift back into the same old cliques as before, because the danger was obvious. He told me some other stuff, as well, saying some of the residents were doing things he thought were unfair.

There was a lot of other stuff too, and it made me feel uneasy. Nobody was supposed to be perfect and it was expected that people would stray to some degree, but that was supposed to be the purpose of the group, and the general pull up system: *Pull your brother up before he pulls you down.*

But I wasn't going to be the one to start blowing covers. I was spending less and less time in the Lodge and felt almost separated from it. The only connection was the information I was getting from *Jason.* He told me all kinds of things, most of which I didn't really want to hear about, but I listened to him anyway.

I felt he needed to get it off his chest. I think he was feeling guilty and hypocritical. I didn't feel too bad myself. I hadn't really been doing anything I wasn't supposed to be doing, with the exception perhaps, of playing the slot machines. The way I saw it, people were going through a treatment system, and even as they got better, we had to understand that they were still people, prone to error. There was nothing wrong with the Lodge's procedures; if anything, they worked, but people were only people, and in the end, they would do what they wanted. All the Lodge could do was point them in the right direction.

It had done that for me. I had come to realise what lay behind my self-destructive streak and my escape into drugs, and I had become a stronger person for it. Now I was ready to move on.

***

It was coming up to Christmas, and I intended to get my own place in the New Year, and put it all behind me. I wasn't earning a lot of money but I wasn't living the high life either. I could make ends meet. I had the company van, too, which was great. It meant I was mobile, and not dependant on public transport.

For the two weeks before Christmas, my boss rented a little shop in Parnell Street, and put me in there selling video games like Pac Man and Space Invaders. It was great to be in town for the hustle and bustle of Christmas. Every evening, after I finished, I collected *Sarah* from work and drove her home. Some evenings, I stayed in her house, watching the telly before driving back to the Lodge. It was almost like old times between us, although we weren't getting intimate; just a quick kiss goodnight at her front door and a 'see you tomorrow.'

One evening before Christmas, *Jason* came into the shop and asked me if I would give him a lift home. He was going to spend a few days there. I agreed, and after collecting *Sarah*, we headed out that way. *Jason's* house was right beside one of the big pubs off the main road to South Dublin. *Sarah* and I had often drunk there years before when she was working in the shopping centre nearby. She suggested going in for a drink and we both agreed. *Jason* dropped his gear into his house and we headed into the pub. I ordered a glass of Harp for *Sarah* and a Coke for myself

'What are you having, *Jason*?' I asked.

'A pint of Guinness,' he said.

'Are you sure?'

'Sure, I'm sure. It's Christmas, isn't it.'

'Then I think I'll have a pint myself,' I said, cancelling the Coke.

The ice had been broken, so to speak, and we ended up spending the whole night there. It was great; the Christmas atmosphere, the gargle—the first for 18 months—*Sarah*, the laughs, the drunkenness, the good old times. I didn't feel guilty for too long; maybe two swallows. I rationalised it as part of the re-entry process, the return to normality. *Jason* confessed that he'd been having a few every weekend. He reckoned everyone else had, as well. This made me feel better.

We went back to *Jason*'s house afterwards, and had a few more. I drove *Sarah* home early in the morning, still half-pissed, but full of the joys of having been passionate with her again, though not quite intimate. I spent Christmas at home in my mother's house, having been reminded by the Lodge's psychologist, to remember our commitment to stay off the drink.

I spent St Stephen's day in *Sarah*'s sister's house, where we had a great time. Life was perfect again.

After Christmas, I found an apartment in Chapelizod, and moved out of the Lodge. I distanced myself from it as much as I could, as I felt really hypocritical sitting in the weekly group, and feeling that I knew too much about what was going on outside of the Group Room and after the pull ups. *Marion* was a trained psychiatrist but she could do little with a bunch of ex-junkies, hanging onto their secrets.

***

I started going back up to my local haunts in Drimnagh— The Bentley, The Long Mile Inn, all my old friends and neighbours. It was like the previous three years hadn't happened.

One night, I decided to pay a visit out to the Lodge as I hadn't been out there for weeks. As I walked in to the phase one house, I detected an air of solemnity, almost. I went into the staff office where *Henry* was sitting, reading a book.

'What's going on?' I asked.

'We had a big General Meeting today.'

A GM was only held when someone who'd split had returned.

'Who split?' I asked.

'*Jason*,' he said.

I was shocked.

'But he's in re-entry,' I said incredulously.

'I know, but he hasn't turned up for work for three weeks, and today he called and said he'd been back shooting dope, and asked if he could come back.'

I couldn't believe my ears. In all the time I'd been there, no-one had ever split from re-entry. My mind was in turmoil. I felt angry, and guilty, and vulnerable. I was thinking, *Shit, this could happen to me.*

I remembered when a guy had come over from a place like ours in New York, and they told us the stories about graduates who had messed up after years of being clean, having become successful businessmen, millionaires even. Some of them had even set up their own private therapy centres for rich clients. They had all fallen into the same trap: 'Just a little recreational drugs; it won't do any harm.'

They'd ended back in the dishpan, with shaved heads, washing dishes.

It hit me then; that I was by no means out of the woods yet. Everything had been going well for me. My life was back on track, *Sarah* was talking to me again, I had a job, and my self respect. But I was vulnerable. At any time I could fall into temptation and find myself thinking about a turn-on, telling myself it would be 'just this once' and that all I was doing was having a bit of harmless fun. I knew that the next thing I'd be aware of was that I was strung out again, and probably facing another list of charges as long as my arm. All it would take was one moment of weakness, one lapse of reason when I would convince myself I was just having a good time. Jesus, junkies are more afraid of living than they are of dying.

I left *Henry's* office knowing who was responsible for *Jason's* plight. I headed for the dishpan.

Jason was leaning over the sink, washing the dishes. They hadn't shaved his head but he was wearing a sign around his neck which said, 'I cannot be believed.' He looked humble and broken. I knew the feeling from my own dishpan contract. I asked him what had happened, and he told me the whole sad story. I asked him the reason for the sign, and he explained that he'd blown a few people's covers at the GM, including mine. He said that a few people on the programme were hanging around with drug users, and sometimes took a drink.

'Then why are they still here?' I asked.

'Because they all denied the allegations,' he said. 'No one believed me. That's why I'm wearing the sign.'

He was feeling really down. He said he'd had a few turn-ons but he hadn't really felt stoned.

'It's true what they say, Shay. I've got too much awareness after being so long in this place. There isn't enough junk out there to get me stoned.'

I said goodbye, telling him to hang on in there. I got into my van and drove away from there, angry and confused. I drove down to my brother's house in Blanchardstown, and told him the whole story. Joey didn't really understand. No-one could really understand unless they had been through it themselves. He just advised me to follow my conscience.

I called *Jamie* and told him I had to talk to him urgently. He invited me up to his house. When I arrived, a guy called *Adam* was there. He was *Jamie*'s confidant and the only former resident in phase three, besides me. I told him I had been up to the Lodge, and found out about *Jason*'s GM. I told him that the allegations he made about me were true. He asked me if I knew if the allegations against the others were true, and I said they would have to answer that question themselves. He told me he'd felt that there was something going on, and so had *Adam*, but they couldn't put their finger on it.

As *Jamie* was at the top of the staff structure, he had more to do than take groups and check everything that was going on in the house. He had to take care of the budgets—the precarious finances of the whole place, and liaising with the Eastern Health Board, The Board of Directors and other Therapeutic Communities throughout the world. Because of the growing numbers of people needing treatment, he was dependent on the staff and the re-entry part-timers to keep the show on the road.

He then asked me if I would say what I'd just said in front of the whole community. I agreed. I didn't want *Jason* to be the only one to take the punishment, especially the sign around his neck, as I knew he was telling the truth.

Jamie rang the bell, signalling everyone to the group room for a GM. He sent *Adam* over to the re-entry house to get anybody who was there over to the group room.

After everybody had assembled, *Jamie* said I had an announcement to make. I stood up and said my piece, admitting that *Jason*'s allegations about me breaking the re-entry house rules regarding drinking alcohol were true; that in my case anyway, he wasn't telling lies. *Jamie* then asked if anybody else from the re-entry house, or any of the staff, had anything to add. They all declined.

Some of the residents in the phase one house expressed their disappointment in me in no uncertain 'Hats Off' terms, saying how much they had previously admired me and saw me as a good example to follow. I felt really small in one way but good in another—unburdened, I suppose. I just wanted to get out of the Lodge and get on with my life.

Jamie congratulated me for being brave enough to make my statement, and expressed a wish that anyone else who had something they wanted to admit to, should do so there and then, or later in a group, before the guilt drove them out of the community.

Nobody confessed, but within a few days some changes were made to the day to day running of the Lodge.

For me, I was glad to be out of the daily politics of the place, but the whole episode of *Jason* leaving and coming back, and ending up as he was, scared me. It showed me that any sort of setback or frustration could lead me to fall back into drugs, and I wasn't sure I would be able to get back out again if that happened. I knew I wasn't really ready to tempt fate and start life back on the streets of Dublin. Maybe I'd be better off heading back to Germany again. I contacted my old boss in the china set scam business and asked if he had any jobs going. In the meantime, I would have to sit tight and keep my mind off drugs.

CHAPTER 15

I never went back to the Lodge. I just kept in touch by phone. I found out that some of the people who had split were back on the gear, and that *Jason* had left again and was doing the same. A lot had gone clean.

It bothered me though, that I might not succeed in staying off heroin. I wondered if I had done the right thing by leaving. It would have been a lot better if we'd been honest with each other earlier, which I thought we all were.

I wasn't making a lot of money in the job, so I gave up my flat and moved back in with my ma. Working on commission only, I was never sure I'd be able to pay the rent. I fell back into the old lifestyle, just going up to the local for a few pints when I could afford it, and even when I couldn't. There was no shortage of people who would buy me a drink.

Some of my old mates were raving alcoholics now. With them, it wasn't just a few pints. It was triple gin and tonics in a half pint glass. I had been sticking to a few—five or six at weekends out of financial necessity, and usually in the quietest of the locals, The Halfway House, or the waiting room for Mount Jerome Cemetery, as it was known.

I drank there because it was a couple of pence cheaper; and I could watch the football and other sporting events on the telly, in the suitable pub atmosphere. I didn't have a lot of suitable friends to choose from, though; not like the last time I had kicked the habit.

At that time, I had hung around with Joey, my younger brother, and all his mates. That was how I had managed to stay clean for four and a half years. Getting back into the football and hurling had helped, too. But that had been back in 1975, when I was 23. Now all the lads were married and living miles away from Drimnagh. It was 1983, and I was 31, and hardly likely to make my way onto any team, except maybe Coolmine itself, against the 'drug squad'.

Most of the local action was in a pub just up the road, but I had been barred before I went into the Lodge. The owners had been advised to bar me by a Special Branch man who lived locally. He'd told him I was a drug addict and criminal, or words to that effect. I'd ventured in a couple of times to see if I'd be served but the answer had always been an emphatic, 'No.' In fairness to them, I was a junkie, and nobody wants a junkie hanging around their pub.

It was nice to be drug free—but it was boring. The highlight of the week was a couple of trips up to the Halfway House for a gargle.

I decided to try the local once more. It was a Thursday night, about 10pm. The place was packed, as the weekend had begun. I wasn't pushed if I they served me or not, but I was hoping to meet someone who might give me a lift up to Taylor's Grange or one of the other popular Thursday night discos in the Dublin Mountains. I didn't want to drive the company van drunk. I was making my way along the bar when I heard a loud shout: 'Shay, great to see you, what are you having?'

It was one of my old mates. He was sitting at the bar with two others. I explained to them that I was barred and had just popped in to see if I could see anyone I knew.

'Don't worry about that Shay. What are you having?'

'A pint,' I said.

He ordered for me and the barman told him I was barred. The three lads decided to right this injustice and insisted on talking to the owner. He was sticking by his word, until they threatened to leave and never drink there again. The round for the lads was three triple gin and tonics, ten times a night—and that four or five nights a week. The owner, being a businessman, reckoned it up quickly, and let me stay.

I had a social life again. Two of these guys were married with kids. The other was single and had a nice four-bedroom house in one of the first estates ever built in Tallaght, at the time when it was still more or less a village. Any of the lads who were having problems with the missus were welcome to cool their heels off in his crib. In fact, everyone was welcome in his crib. It was famous for the outlandish parties—or should I say orgies—that had been going on there for years.

I had known these guys since school. They were a couple of years older than me and liked a bit of dope, and when they could get their hands on it, the odd line of coke or smack. But 90% of the time, they were party animals, and I was badly in need of a party.

I stayed on the pints that night, just glad to be back in the fold. I was excused from the round due to my lack of funds; in fact, I didn't have to pay for anything all night. I had great craic for the first time in years. We went to Taylor's and then back to the infamous house to continue the party.

I woke up the next morning with a woeful hangover, made worse by the fact that the Coolmine philosophies were running round in my head. I was highly aware that this was not the type of behaviour that would keep me on the straight and narrow. But I managed to rationalise it all away. Sure, hadn't I spent many a night in my friend's house getting locked when I was off the junk before, and I'd never gotten into anything else, not even when they'd been having a blow or snorting a line of coke. If I could do it then, I could do it now.

It was party time all the time after that.

Then one day, while sleeping off a hangover in this guy's house, I heard a bit of hassle downstairs. I crept over to the window and saw a green Jag parked outside. It was a fella I knew, a motorcycle courier. Himself and my old school mate were having a heated discussion downstairs. All sorts of scenarios were running through my mind, not least of which was the worry that the house would be raided for some reason. I didn't need that, not now, not while I was there. I'd only been given probation because I was in the Lodge. If I was caught there with a deal going down, it was back to square one. I waited until the discussion had ended and I heard the car driving away. After what I thought was a suitable time, I made my way downstairs and having bid adieu, made my way down to my mother's, relieved.

I had to get out. Luckily, I saw some more ads in the *Irish Times* newspaper, looking for sales people in Germany, and I knew my chance to make a fresh start had come. I applied, and within a couple of weeks I was ready to pack my bags and go, leaving Dublin and its drug epidemic behind.

***

I started off initially with the same china tea set business I had been involved with the first time I was in Germany, but I soon chucked it in. I hung around Frankfurt for a few weeks after I'd finished, in the hope of finding a job, but to no avail, and had spent most of the time in the 24-hour 'drink merry-go-round' that was Frankfurt Sachsenhausen: a pedestrianised area with lots of pubs and restaurants, each with a different ethnic theme. It was a great place to meet people, and of course there was more than one Irish bar.

I ended up living with my sister for a while, in Sindelfingen, looking for a new job. It was great for the first couple of weeks; nice to be involved with a family life, getting to know my nieces in their own environment. I'd previously only seen them while they were on holidays in Ireland.

I had no better success finding a job in Sindelfingen then I had in Frankfurt. It was a lot less fun, too. My days consisted of trips to the Labour Exchange and writing job applications. I didn't feel bad living off my sister and she never made me feel bad about it. She was glad to have a member of the family living with her, but I felt terrible when she had to include cigarettes and beer on her daily shopping list, as neither she nor Wolfgang smoked or drank, and were very careful with their expenditure.

I was out of a job, but I knew I couldn't chance going home yet. I wanted to stay away from Dublin and all the people who brought back too many bad memories, and too many temptations. At the same time, I knew I couldn't, and didn't want to, just sponge off my sister indefinitely, so after a while I headed off again and spent a few weeks living over one of the Irish pubs in Frankfurt Sachsenhausen.

This Irish pub was the most popular pub in the whole area, mainly because of the live music every night. Over the pub, there was a room for the musicians. It was part of their deal as it saved the hotel bill. It also doubled as a doss house for everybody who arrived in Frankfurt without a tosser—and oddly enough there were quite a few of them.

A lot of people were coming and going, some deciding that this wasn't the life for them and heading back to Ireland, but this was not an option for me. I knew things hadn't changed a great deal in Dublin since I'd left.

I knew that if I went home I would be back on the gear all too soon. It was far too early for me to walk back into the lion's den.

Another reason why I decided to stick around was that *Sarah* was living there at that stage, having made a spontaneous decision to pack up and move to Germany. We weren't seeing eye to eye, but I hoped all that could change.

She had arrived over in Frankfurt a few months earlier, just after Christmas. I'd been on the road doing the china after the Christmas break, and had called her to wish her a Happy New Year. Her sister had told me she was in Frankfurt, and staying with a friend. I was shocked, and wondered why she had chosen to come to Germany. I wanted to believe it was because of me but that didn't make a great deal of sense. There'd been years of her totally ignoring me when I was back on the gear, and just the brief period together which had followed my time in the Lodge.

Maybe I had another chance after all. Maybe the years spent apart had made her realise she couldn't live without me.

I called the number her sister had given me, and arranged to meet her on a Sunday to talk things over. She agreed, and gave me directions to her apartment on the opposite side of the river to Sachsenhausen. I had butterflies in my stomach as I approached her front door, as I hadn't laid eyes on her for six months, and when I did, she looked as good as ever.

CHAPTER 16

While I was waiting for a decent job to come along, I did some work with a guy called *Bo*. Among his many talents, he was a dab hand at making an Irish stew. He'd cook it at the weekends and sell it to all the lads he'd been sending out to build things all over the Reich during the week. He'd also sell it to the Yanks who'd pour into the pub at the weekends. His sales pitch was beautiful: 'Here. Eat this. Five marks please.'

I helped *Bo* with the stew. I didn't know if I was going up or down in the world, and to be honest, I really didn't care. I didn't know the difference. All I knew was that I was no longer on heroin. *Bo*, however, felt my talents were wasted selling stew, and so he introduced me to some English guys who were selling cars to the Yanks. They all stormed the Irish pub at the weekends, and one of them, *Tel*, said he'd arrange an interview for me.

After that, it was all plain sailing for a while. I got the job, and found that just as I had done with the china sets, I seemed to have a flair for selling to the Americans, only this

237

time it was cars. I felt really lucky, for a change. I was given cash up front and a company car, followed by more cash.

I was delighted for myself, and told all the people who had been taking care of me since I had left the china business about my newfound success.

There were a few formalities I had to go through though, before I became an official car salesman. I might have started to panic at this stage, thinking that my less than stellar past might come back to haunt me, but the way I was looking at things—positively for a change—I thought it was a good thing; a sign that this was a legitimate, good job with prospects.

I had to register with the authorities in Germany, which had been a complete 'no no' in the china business. I was told also to get a *Polizeifuhrungszeugnis* or police report from the local German police. I felt it would have been wiser of them to get this before they gave us the car and the money, but I didn't tell them that.

I wasn't too worried about the police report. Although I had been arrested by the American MP's hundreds of times while selling the china, the German police had always let us go. I was given a couple more checks for 900 Deutschmarks each, and one for 3,000. A couple of days later, I received another check, for 3,000. I'd been with the company for only ten days, and before I'd even started working, I had already received more than 14,000 Deutschmarks. I hadn't had so much money since I'd been picking pockets.

One day after a sales meeting, I came home to find a letter from the police waiting for me, and I knew it was the police report. I tore it open and saw that there was something written on it. I couldn't understand it so I brought it to one of the barmen in the pub, who could read German, and he told me it meant I had a conviction for trespassing on an American base. I was devastated.

Everything had been going so well, and now this. I had visions of losing my job, the car, and having to pay back all the advances. I couldn't quite get into the weekend like I'd anticipated and to make matters worse, *Bo* introduced me to a load of salesmen who were all regaling me with their tales of how much they were earning—ten, 15 and even 20,000 Deutschmarks a month. I could see my chance slipping away. A police clearance was essential.

I talked it over with my boss and we found a solution, which involved me working out of a different sales area. It would be tougher, but I was determined to make a go of my new life, so I decided that I would go along with what had to be done. I got on with the job.

'Hey Joe, how about a nice new car today?'

I didn't particularly want to leave Frankfurt, as all my mates were there. *Sarah* was still there, too, and maybe the new job would change things between us. I hoped we could make things work. The best times we'd had together were when I'd been working in a proper job. But I knew I had to leave Sachsenhausen and luckily I was offered a nice place which was handy for work. I really felt that my life was getting better. I bought furniture—TV, stereo, the whole shebang. I had a home of my own, and I felt proud.

Everyone was glad for me that I'd landed on my feet but it remained to be seen if I would stay on them.

***

Things were getting better between myself and *Sarah* too, and we would meet up most weekends and have a few drinks. After a while, the inevitable happened and we started going out as a couple again. We did 'couple things' together, and she started buying things for my apartment. The hectic lifestyle in Sachsenhausen was beginning to get to her though, as it did to most of the people who lived there for any length of time.

Combined with this, our romance, which had faltered so many times over the years, just didn't seem strong enough to hold us together any more. We argued a lot, and found that we had both changed so much since we had first been together, and eventually the relationship just fizzled out. It was devastating because I had thought she was the love of my life, but it wasn't to be. I knew this because it was not long after we split up that I met the true love of my life; my wife.

***

It was August 1988 and I was standing in the beer garden in the Irish pub in Nürnberg, where my sales manager was holding a meeting. I had been salesman of the month for three months running, and it looked like I was going to make it four in a row. I felt like I was on a roll, so when the meeting ended I walked over to where she was sitting and just started talking to her.

I had noticed her arrival and felt instantly attracted to her, and after I attempted a few dodgy phrases in bad German, she told me she could speak English. Her name was Ute, and I found out that she was really nice and very easy to get along with.

Neither of us wanted to end the night when the pub closed, so we headed off to a club and eventually went back to her place, where we slept side by side, but without doing anything. When we woke up the next morning I asked her if she would see me again, and she said yes. I knew we would see a lot of each other after that.

I was over the moon to be getting on so well; a good job, potential for promotion, money and now a beautiful girlfriend, but I was about to hit an obstacle that could have ruined it all for me. I had a breakdown.

***

I had arranged a big party to celebrate the major upturn in my life, because I just felt so happy about the way things were going. It wasn't that much of a distant memory to remember my days of squalor and crime, when I was at the lowest point of my life, shooting up gear whenever I got the chance and robbing every single day just to get enough to score.

I decided to invite *Jamie* from the Lodge over, because in a way I wanted to show my peers, the people I knew had gone through the same things as me, that I had successfully beaten heroin addiction and was now making something of my life. I found out later that he was bringing another guy who had gone through Coolmine with him, but didn't think there was any harm in it.

I was just reaching a successful end to a very difficult year. No one had thought I would make it as a successful salesman, but I had. I had made sure to develop a good team of sales people and had made good contacts with our finance department in the New York office. This was essential to getting the deal done quickly. I could do a deal in the morning, and have the customer driving the same day.

I had moved into a new apartment in the nicest part of Nürnberg city centre. I was on a roll, and nothing could hold me back. It had been a tough year but I had weathered the storm. I was back to my old self.

The lead up to the day of the party was chaotic. A guy I had taken under my wing had turned out to be nothing but trouble, and had caused us to lose a huge amount of sales at a time when it really mattered. Not content with this, he had then taken a company car and driven to his old job, where he had shouted abuse at the owners and staff. I had to go and collect him from the police station. Then I had to sort out a place for *Jamie*'s friend to stay. I also had to make sure all the usual stuff was prepared; glasses, seats, food, and everything else.

I had to eventually bring the guy who took the company car to a doctor, because it was quite clear he wasn't playing with a full deck of cards, and I had to reassure his mother back in Ireland that he was OK and was being looked after.

I then had to go to the airport and pick up *Jamie* and his friend on the day of the party, but due to a military parade blocking traffic, I ended up being hours late, by which time they had both had more than a few drinks. *Jamie*'s friend was fast asleep. We drove back, but still couldn't wake the guy up when we got there. He was dead to the world, so we headed around to the pub, about 100 yards away. We agreed that someone would go back and check on him every few minutes.

I wanted a chance to talk to *Jamie* alone, but it was impossible as the pub was packed. I was hoping *Jamie* would be impressed with me and put his imprimatur on my success before the weekend was over. He was my only peer. I was doing my best to tell *Jamie* who everybody was, and introduce him to some of my friends, colleagues and managers.

I had just finished my third beer when one of the guys rushed in.

'Shay, come quickly. The police are up at your car talking to your mate.'

We rushed around the corner, and sure enough, there was a squad car parked beside the car. They were interviewing *Jamie*'s friend, and there was glass all over the path. He was in no position to talk even if he'd been able to understand the language, as he was still half locked. I introduced myself to the policeman, and asked him what the problem was. He explained that someone had called in to say there had been a report of a broken window in the car, and upon investigating it they had found him inside. They had determined that the window had been broken from inside, and were asking him if he could shed any light on what had happened, as they weren't confronted too often by a car break out.

I asked the guy what had happened, and he said he couldn't remember. After the police had left, he explained that he had woken up, totally disorientated, and couldn't get the doors open or even open the window, as the car had central locking and power windows, and he had no key. So he had kicked the window in instead, as he felt trapped.

He insisted then that he didn't want to go to another pub, as he had had enough to drink—it had been his first drink in over a year. He just wanted to go to my place and sleep. I explained to him that my place was a two hour drive away, and I planned to go to a party. I told him it would be great, with lots of girlies, nice food, cola, but no matter what I said, he kept on insisting on going to my place. *Jamie* didn't know what to say, as he had invited this guy, and now he was ruining my whole plan for the weekend.

The guy was angry and totally unreasonable, and although he was very small, he was, by reputation, capable of some damage, if aroused. Whatever he had drunk at the airport had turned him into a monster, and I could see why he'd been abstaining from the demon in Ireland. He was obnoxious.

'You'se are trying to set me up,' he started.

We were all astounded. We didn't know what he was on about.

'Cool it. No one is trying to set you up,' *Jamie* was saying, just as his friend leaped out of his seat and loafed me right on the nose. I was too stunned to react. I felt my nose. It wasn't broken. There was no blood. He hadn't managed to connect properly as he had jumped over the front seat to connect with me in the back.

'This is all your fault,' he said, addressing me. Everyone was flabbergasted.

One of the guys I knew who had come out to see what had happened had jumped out of the way in fright. He didn't know what was going on. I had been telling him all about Coolmine, and the benefits of therapy; how it helps people to change their behaviour and how a bit of therapy might not be bad for him. And now he was looking at a total nutcase who had been to Coolmine himself. This was the old version—the one before the change—who had loafed me in the head and kicked in the window. I didn't try to fight back or anything, I was hurt and disappointed. These were my peers, and one of them had totally flipped out.

I didn't realise it at the time, but looking back, it was probably just then that I snapped too.

I was no longer in the mood for a party, so I called Ute and asked if I could stay with her, and she agreed. I was simmering, full of anger and disappointment, but I wasn't letting it show.

I drove *Jamie* and his friend back to the airport on Monday morning, with the guy I'd been looking after also with me, but instead of returning to work to get on with my new life, I just kept going. I disappeared for the day. It was like I was back on the gear, living in an altered state somewhere between being awake and asleep, in a sort of noddy-land where nothing really mattered and reality was none of my business.

'Where to?' my colleague asked.

'Around the car park,' I replied.

I had a million things to do and I was running out of time to do them all. We drove round and round the car park, maybe for half an hour, maybe an hour. Eventually I said, 'Let's get out of here.'

'Where to?' he asked again.

'Anywhere, let's go.'

I sat in the back beside the broken window, with the jacket covering the hole. I felt like a priest in a confession box, a mobile confession box. My colleague drove.

He just drove and drove. When we were close to running out of gas, he'd pull over and tank up on my Mastercard. There were some nice sounds on the radio and people were singing me messages. I was to keep on going.

I called my office and asked someone to sing 'My Way' for me.

'I can't. I'm with a customer. Where are you?'

'I'm in a car. I'll call you back.'

'What's your number? I'll call *you* back.'

'I don't know the number. I'll call you back.'

Later, I called the New York office. It was in Long Island but I told her to look out the window and asked her if she could see the Empire State Building. When I knew she had it in view, I sang her a few refrains of 'Fly Me to the Moon'. When I was finished she asked me if I was alright. I told her I'd never felt better in my life. She asked me where I was. I told her I honestly didn't know.

I spoke to everybody on the phone, sometimes singing them a song. I asked my colleague to call people too. We were a team now, like Batman and Robin. We drove to his old job to right whatever wrongs had been done to him. He called his mother and told her everything was OK; he was with Shay.

Just before the autobahn, as daylight was approaching, we parked beside this old house. I knew I'd come back here. It was a beautiful sunrise. I told him to pull over onto the lay by. He did, and I climbed up on the bonnet, hands outstretched to greet the sun. I had never seen it like this before. It was breathtaking. My colleague put the car in gear. It lurched forward and I fell backwards, my arse in the middle of the windscreen. It shattered but didn't break. There were loads of tiny broken bits in the middle of the windscreen. When I climbed back inside, the sunrise looked even better, multiplied a million prismatic times. He drove.

For days.

Everyone was trying to find us, but we weren't lost. Now every time I called someone, their phones were busy. When I did manage to reach someone, they weren't listening. They just wanted to ask questions:

'Where are you?'

'Where were you?'

'What are you doing?'

'Why are you doing this?'

'When will you be back in the office?'

'When will you be home?'

'Where can we contact you?'

'What's your number?'

Questions, questions, questions. I didn't know the answers anymore, and no one wanted to listen to me sing. My colleague drove on.

I started counting the souls of people. I could tell the difference between the good ones and the bad ones. I upset somebody, because soon there were two policemen in their green jackets and beige pants and white hats with black guns and holsters, and before I knew it I was sitting handcuffed in an underground police station. Some hours later, they let me go, after a doctor had told them I was fine.

I went back to the office with my colleague. I walked around looking for something, but not knowing what I was looking for. Everyone I met looked shocked, and I didn't know why. I was the number one salesman and was going to break all records. I didn't fit. They tried to keep me there, trap me, because I didn't fit. It wouldn't make sense to the others in the sales force if I didn't fit—Salesman of the Year. I knew what they wanted. They thought they had me, but I wouldn't stay. They even came with me in the lift. They looked scared; they wanted to hold me. I knew this, but they were afraid to touch me because I was lost, losing, a loser. I might be contagious.

I left, and headed to the Irish pub, where my brother Johnny finally located and collected me. I was glad to see him. He drove me to his apartment, loading me down with questions I couldn't answer. I was really tired and he was being aggressive with me, telling me he had been chasing after me for days, as had loads of other people. He told me of all the money people had lost because of me. We were in his place now, and he was making phone calls to various people. I could hear him telling people I was safe, and no, I couldn't talk right now. He wanted to understand what had happened. It was impossible to explain. I was lying on the bed trying to get some sleep. He told me it was Thursday. I could see and feel and hear the devil outside the window.

Early in the morning he took me to the doctor. I started to bark in his surgery. He got the message. He prepared a syringe full of pink liquid. I looked at it and said, 'That's exactly what I need.'

Then he stuck it in me. Nobody was driving anymore.

***

I woke up groggily. I was surrounded by empty beds—hospital I guessed. I was wearing a white smock, tied at the back. I was naked otherwise. Someone came into the room and I covered my arse with the blanket I'd kicked off, and rolled over onto my back.

'*Servus!*' he greeted me. He was Bavarian or Austrian.

'*Schön genug geschlaffen?*' He wanted to know if I'd slept enough. I had no idea. I still felt sleepy. He was between 25 and 28, with long black hair and a moustache. He was wearing jeans, cowboy boots and a colourful hand knit sweater. He looked happy.

'*Brauchst Du was zum anziehen?*'

I felt naked in the smock and said, '*Ja, Ich weiß nicht wo meine kleider sind.*'

He threw me a pair of jeans, some socks and a t-shirt.

'*Du bist kein Deutscher.*'

He'd noticed from my couple of sentences that I wasn't German. He had addressed me in the familiar *du* form. He obviously didn't stand on ceremony.

'Where are you from?' he continued.

'Ireland. How long have I been asleep?'

'Since you arrived two days ago.' he said.

'Where are we?' I asked.

'The psychiatric hospital in Lohr am Main.'

Psychiatric hospital, I was thinking to myself, *why am I here?* I looked around the room. No one looked crazy. Some of them looked sad, preoccupied even. The rest of them looked in good spirits, but no one looked crazy.

I was trying to remember. I remembered Johnny bringing me to the doctor. That was it. The doctor thought I was crazy. I thought that it was a bit like being back in Coolmine, with the same sad faces and lack of memories of years of our lives, except we didn't have to wash the dishes or anything.

After a couple of weeks, I got released. Ute collected me. Remarkably. I had only known her for six weeks at that stage, and yet she had stood by me. It wouldn't be the last time.

I went back to Ute's place, but having recovered from whatever it was that had happened to me, I began to see the grim reality of the situation once more. My job was certainly gone, I had probably lost all of my friends and colleagues, and I had little chance of getting another job in the short term. Also, rather worryingly, I had discovered that my mind was not as strong as it used to be. Years of heroin abuse had obviously taken their toll, leaving me slightly fragile at times.

Ute had a good job and I just hung around all day while she worked. I spent hours on the phone, trying to get through to the office, trying to sort out my paycheck, as I had no income any more. Everyone I spoke to told me about some of the crazy shit I'd done and I was ashamed. It was like I had just come off heroin all over again.

I gave up my apartment and ended up moving into Ute's place, and to say I was grateful to her for her kindness would be an understatement. I couldn't believe how supportive she was. In the few weeks I had known her, I had gone from a successful salesman with big ambitions to a raving lunatic, and then a humbled, vulnerable, unemployed man with no prospects. It must have been love.

CHAPTER 17

After a while I managed to get myself a new job, again in car sales, and started helping Ute out with the bills. We had grown very close very quickly, and as I told her about my past and what I had gone through, she listened and understood with sympathy. She wasn't thrilled by my wild tales, but she knew I was trying my best to turn my life around. She felt I had, and that I had since overcome another setback when I had recovered from my breakdown.

It was hard to start at the bottom again, having been so successful in my previous job, but I knew there was a price to pay for my past, and that I might never know the full extent of the damage I had done to myself. Two guys from Dublin I had introduced to the business were driving Porsches while I was stuck with an old jeep, which I eventually had to sell to tide me over.

I knew I wasn't doing brilliantly anymore, but as far as I was concerned, I was doing OK. I had a loving, steady relationship, and I was well and truly over my addiction. I had people who cared for me, but what was more, I wanted to be cared for by those people.

In the past I had nearly destroyed myself in an effort to distance myself from my loved ones, to keep them at an arm's length, because I didn't want to face losing anybody ever again after my da died. I wanted no part of reality back then, but I realised now that it was ordinary life that was so precious; an idea I had missed back when I was shooting gear every day.

***

I would soon learn that there was even more for me to care about. Ute and I were having dinner in a restaurant when she broke the news to me that she was pregnant. I was shocked, delighted, and proud. I would be a father. I hadn't imagined that in a million years I could be a father!

I became more determined than ever to make a success of my life from that point on, and over the next few months my sales record improved dramatically. I was making good money again.

On 9 August 1989, exactly one year after we had met, Ute was admitted to hospital and gave birth to Patrick, my first son. There were complications for Ute but after a scare and a medical procedure, she was fine. The two people I loved more than anything else were healthy, and I was close to tears with joy.

It had been such a turnaround from only a few years before when there wasn't a single person in the world I could honestly say I loved more than heroin. Back then I would have done anything to score. Now, I had other, far more important, and far better things to care about.

***

Things weren't always smooth after that, and I have faced a few reminders of just how much damage has been done to my nervous system and my brain. After so many years of drug abuse, poisoning my veins with scag, and poisoning my mind with stupid, self-deluding junkie logic about not needing anyone and living outside of reality, I am prone to moments of weakness.

A few days after Christmas 1990, Ute had to call the emergency doctor for me as I had gone once more into breakdown mode. I remember I'd been holding Patrick in my arms in the wintergarden, and thought I was the Madonna with baby Jesus. I felt I was being told to throw Jesus out the window. It was only for a second, but any parent can imagine just how frightening a thought that is—thinking, even for a second, that that is the right thing to do.

I felt Saddam Hussein's addresses to the world media on the television were personal messages for me.

The emergency doctor never asked me about any of this stuff, and having spoken to Ute about my medical history, gave me a jab so I could get some sleep. I'd been awake for days. When I woke up, I felt better. It had been a bad Christmas. I was later diagnosed with unipolar disorder, which can be controlled. Whereas heroin had kept me outside of reality, now I have to make sure that I stay within reality at all times, and there is no place I would rather be.

I left my job, because I thought it might have been playing on my mind too much, but now that I had a wife and kid to look after I knew I needed a new one pretty soon. The evil thoughts in my head started urging me to just pack it all in, leave, get the fuck out of Dodge, leave Ute and Patrick behind and score some gear, get stoned, and live out my days.

But I was too old and wise to listen to that now. I wasn't 16 anymore. I was close to 40, with responsibilities; too old for the streets, too old to get stoned, too old to forget. I had what life was worth living for; a loving partner and a son. There was no way I was going to give all that up for a bag of dope.

I knew I could claw my way back up and make a go of things again. I'd made it back before. After Coolmine, I'd arrived in Germany without a penny. I was making £35,000 a year by 1985, without stealing or getting stoned. I had done it again in 1987 when I lost my job after my breakdown but within a year, I was a top salesman again. I could do it again. I was sure I could do it again.

I'd been told in the hospital not to get involved with anything stressful, but being ill didn't make the bills go away, and it was not an acceptable excuse for the bank.

'Excuse me, but can we just forget about everything, as I'm suffering from unipolar affective disorder.'

It just didn't work like that. I used to fool myself into thinking it would, but now I knew better. I started working in various sectors, and brought in a good wage, which helped a lot when Ute and I married and were later blessed for the second time, as Patrick was joined by a younger brother, Martin.

Since then I have taught English to German students, and have forged a successful new career for myself. It is now nearly 25 years since I left Ireland; 25 years since I left heroin behind, and every day is like a special gift from

God. I am surrounded by loved ones, after so many years of pushing those who cared for me away.

I didn't want to love anybody, and didn't want to be loved. All I wanted was to get stoned, live like I wanted to live, and not care about anybody or anything. But I have learned the error of my ways, and am looking forward to the rest of my life, free from drugs. When I look back over everything that has happened to me, how I lived for so long, how I nearly died, I can't help but feel that there was some sort of miracle at play.

It was a miracle I was not killed back in Fatima Mansions, it was a miracle I managed to get out of the heroin trap, and it has been a miracle that I have finally managed to find the peace and happiness I craved for years.